AF574147

DRAWING AND PAINTING FLOWERS

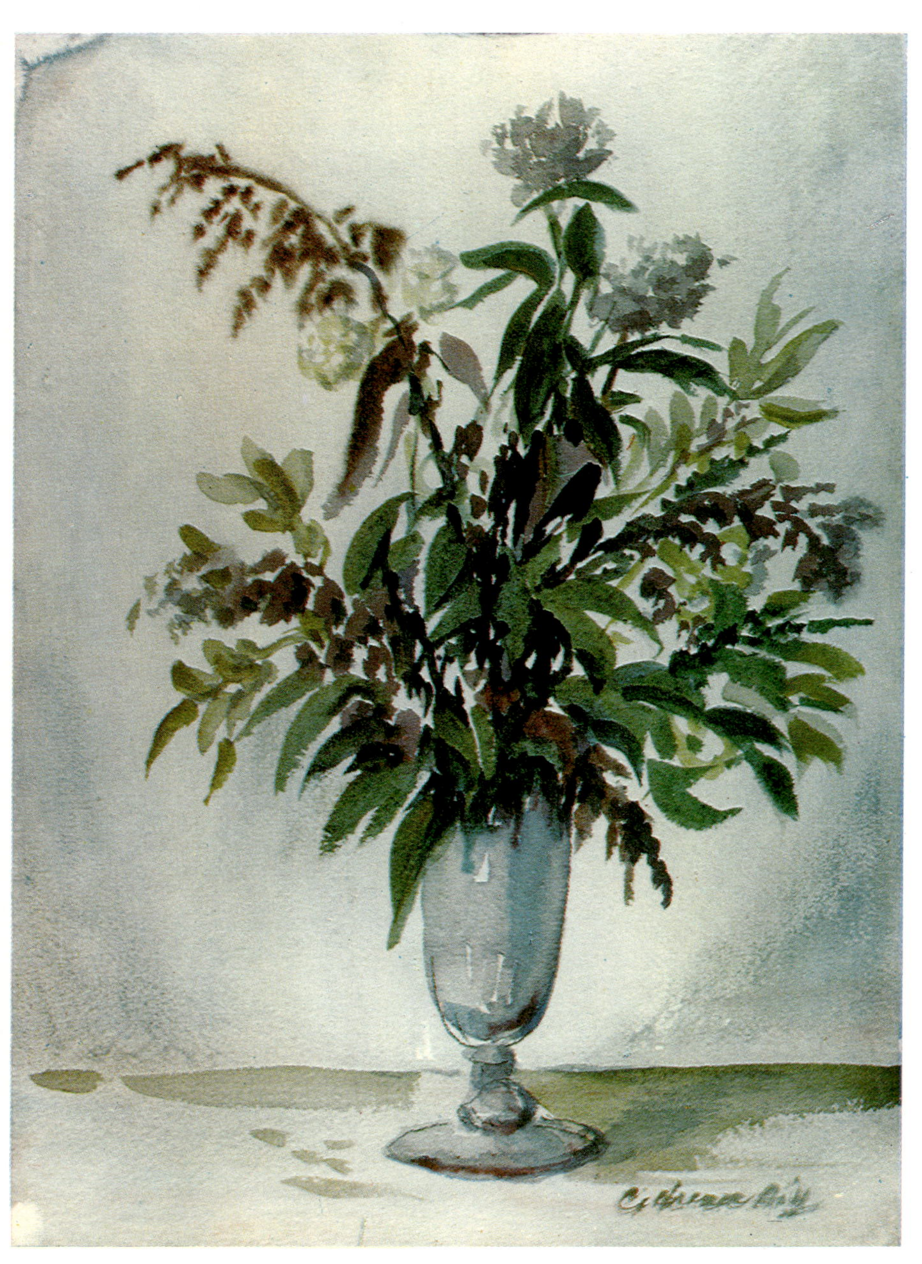

MAINLY FOLIAGE *Swift Study in Watercolour*

The Beginner's Book of

DRAWING AND PAINTING FLOWERS

Written and illustrated by

ADRIAN HILL

P.P.R.O.I. R.B.A.

BLANDFORD PRESS

POOLE DORSET

Blandford Press Ltd
Link House, West Street,
Poole, Dorset BH15 1LL
Reprinted 1977

Made and printed in Great Britain by
Butler & Tanner Ltd, Frome and London

For DOROTHY MARGARET
in very truth, without whom . . .

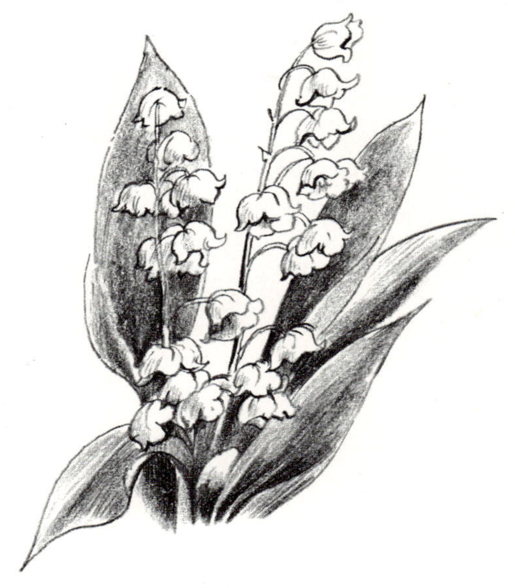

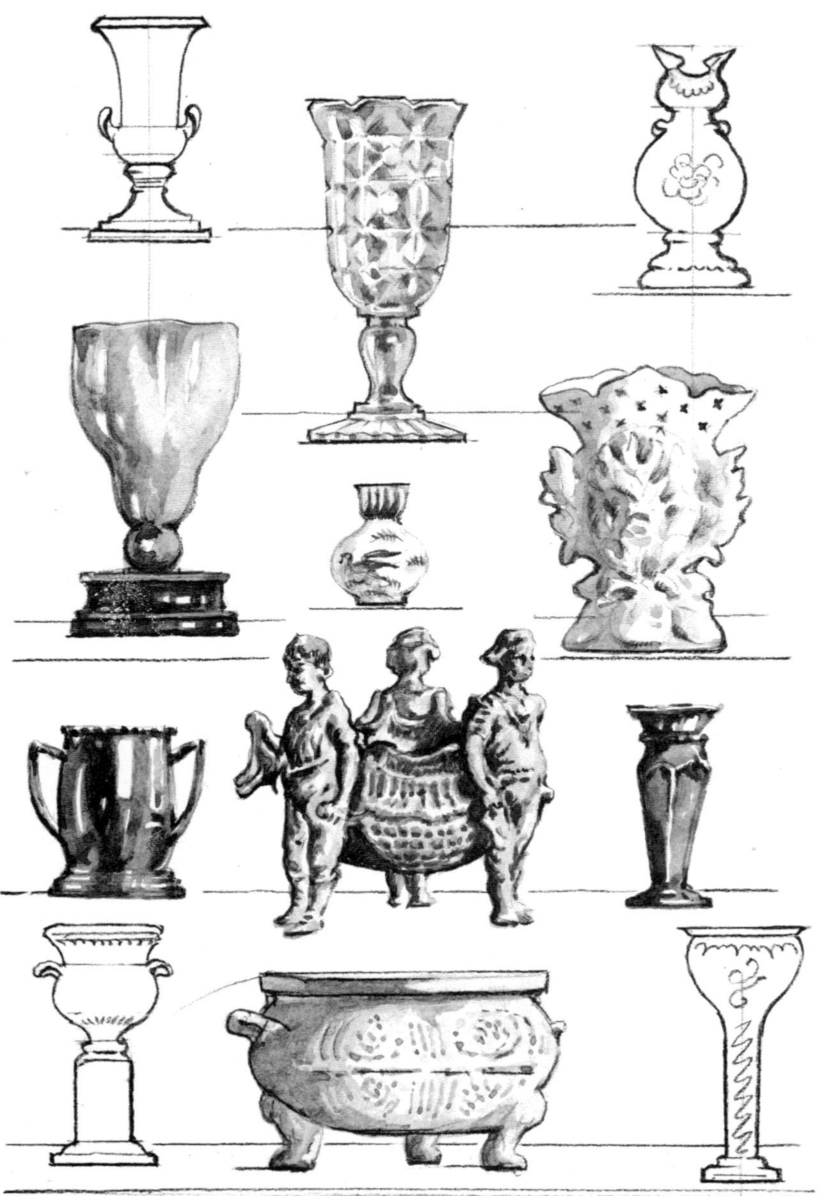

A variety of containers

CONTENTS

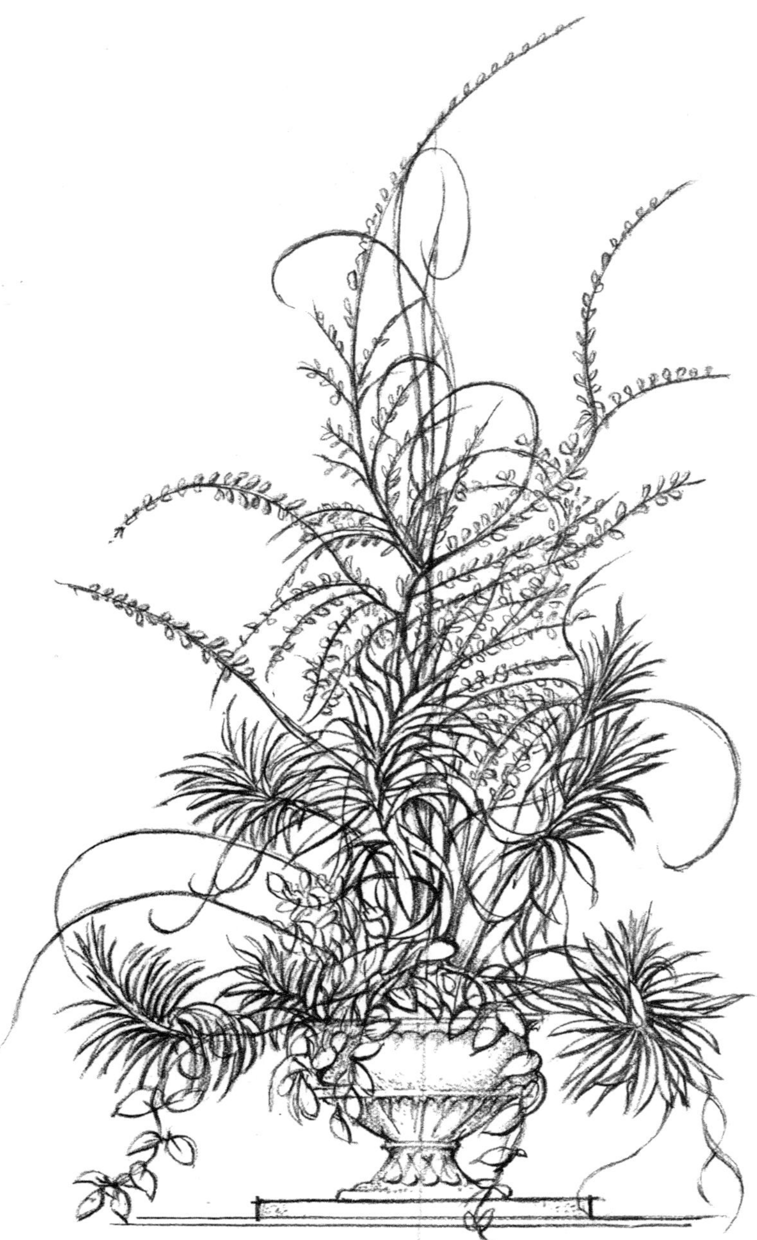

Fine line drawing emphasizes the decorative tracery of this arrangement

LIST OF COLOUR PLATES

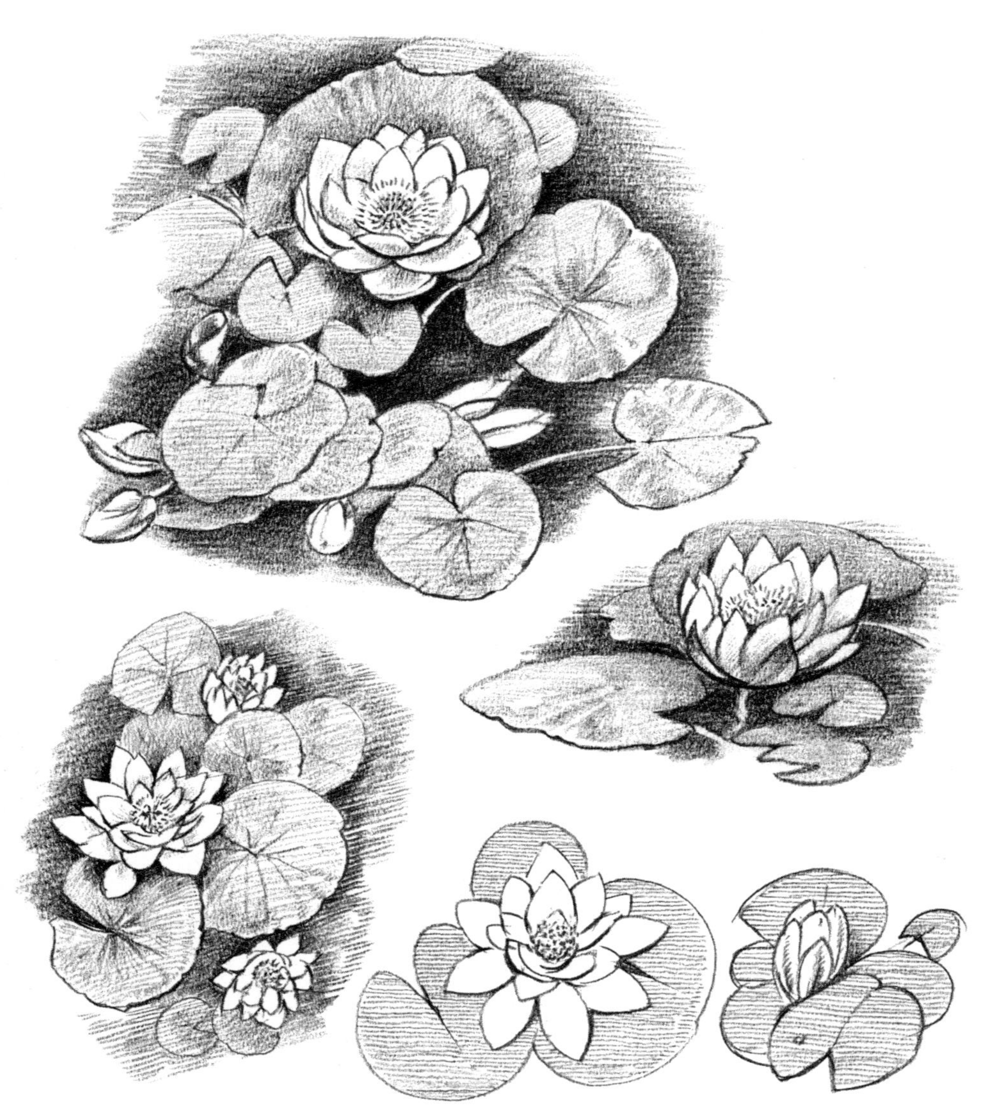

WATER LILIES

INTRODUCTION

IT IS not necessary to be a botanist or a horticulturist to be able to paint flowers. At least I hope not, for I am neither. What I do know is that just as soon as you begin painting flowers, your interest and curiosity will grow, for the more you concentrate on this absorbing study, the more you learn to admire and understand flower habits while realizing their pictorial value. Like human beings and trees, flowers display rich and varied personalities and develop in divers ways. Whilst most species take very kindly to portraiture, others prove in my experience stubbornly unpaintable. Only by trial and error will the reader learn which to approach and which, like other manifestations of Nature, such as sunsets, to be content to admire only!

It often happens that certain flowers, like humans reluctant to pose as models, take kindly to being portrayed *en masse*. While some respond to a robust and romantic treatment, others only reveal their true character when depicted with scrupulous precision. And it is often only by a change of medium, rather than the purely technical approach, that the problem of a successful portrayal is finally resolved.

Certain it is that the frontiers of flower painting have recently advanced and widened both in approach and in the purely technical handling of the subject.

Whereas there are several distinct schools of flower painting—the realistic, the impressionistic, the decorative and the botanical—each in turn calls for a special technique or medium—such as oil, watercolour, pencil or pen and tinted wash. These I hope to deal with under their separate headings. I propose to discuss also the appropriateness of these several mediums and the type of flowers which respond best to each. If I do not include pastel, it is not because I consider it unsuitable for our purpose—on the contrary—but never having indulged myself in this particular medium, I feel it safer to venture to preach only what I practise!

I have given a wide range of drawings in this book for it is only by these details that I am able to support my plea for preliminary study. They also show the marvellous variety of flower size, shape and design at the painter's disposal, the construction of which when properly understood justifies the freedom of a personal approach.

And as there is a tendency to neglect the art of flower arrangement, I have included a number of examples by which I hope to draw attention to some basic rules which govern pattern, outline, balance and colour harmony, because none of these qualities can be overlooked if your painting is to be acceptable to the floral expert as well as to the discriminating eye of the connoisseur of flower painting. For just as a portrait painter sees that his sitter composes well against the right background, so our flower models should have the same consideration in order that they may be displayed to the best advantage.

In these days, flower painting has a wide range which can include "The opulent manipulations of the eye deceiving detail" by the Dutch painters as well as the delicate and lyrical impressionism of the French school, and in this sense flower pictures are on the whole even more appreciated today than they were half a century ago. In the following chapter we can trace the progress that has been made down the ages.

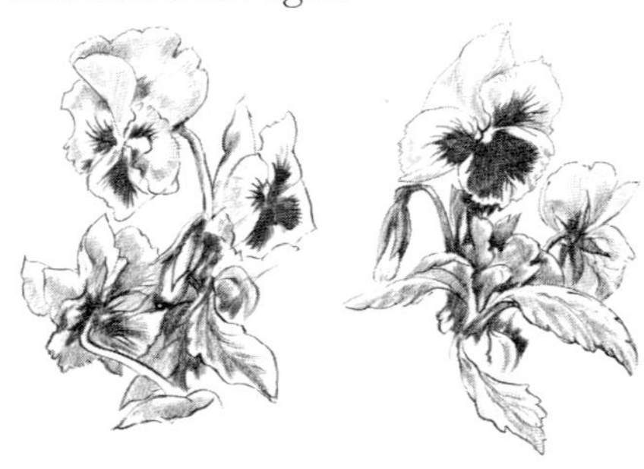

PANSIES

To Mary

with love from

Peter

xxx

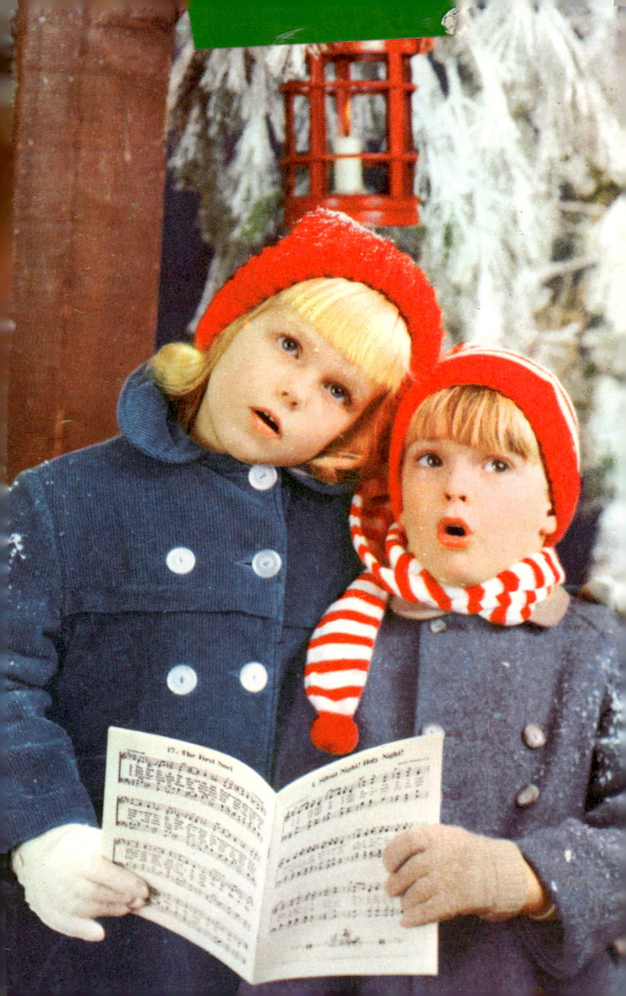
17. The First Noel
1. Silent Night! Holy Night!

1: FLOWER PAINTING DOWN THE AGES

A glance into the past is sufficient to remind us that flower painting has had a long and distinguished, if somewhat checkered, history.

Recent excavations of Pompeian wall paintings have disclosed subjects of garden and flower motifs, the style of painting representing these being described as *opus topiarium*. In these *vividari* Art and Nature are seen to join forces with the happiest effect.

And it is also known that the earliest flower drawings go back nearly two thousand years, from the crude scratchings of the palaeolithic man. In course of time these drawings continued to improve and develop until they were eventually used as illustrations to assist the herbalist, where great realism was required and was to a great degree achieved.

As so often happens, however, these drawings gradually deteriorated from being accurate copies to becoming stylized decorations to the text. A revival of Naturalism did not arrive in fact until the Renaissance, when the flower painter came into his own, recording the rare blooms in the gardens of the stately homes. The truly great flower painters who followed were those who found beauty in truth and who, while understanding and admiring flowers from the botanical angle, yet portrayed them with the discerning eye and accomplished hand of the artist.

During this time such painters flourished in England, France, Germany and especially in Holland, examples of whose richly painted flower pieces can be found in many of our national collections. It is interesting here to note what a number of different kinds of flowers they deemed necessary to composing their opulent paintings. For example in Van Huyson's grandiose "Vase with Flowers" (National Gallery) we can distinguish Peonies, Poppies, Iris, Hollyhocks, Apple Blossom, Narcissus and other late spring and early summer flowers.

Examples of other grandiloquent flower paintings in which the varied and magnificent (if over-blown) blooms cascade all over some ornamental vase or urn are typical of the works produced by Jan Van Os, Reeysch, Brussel and Hem. Executed with great

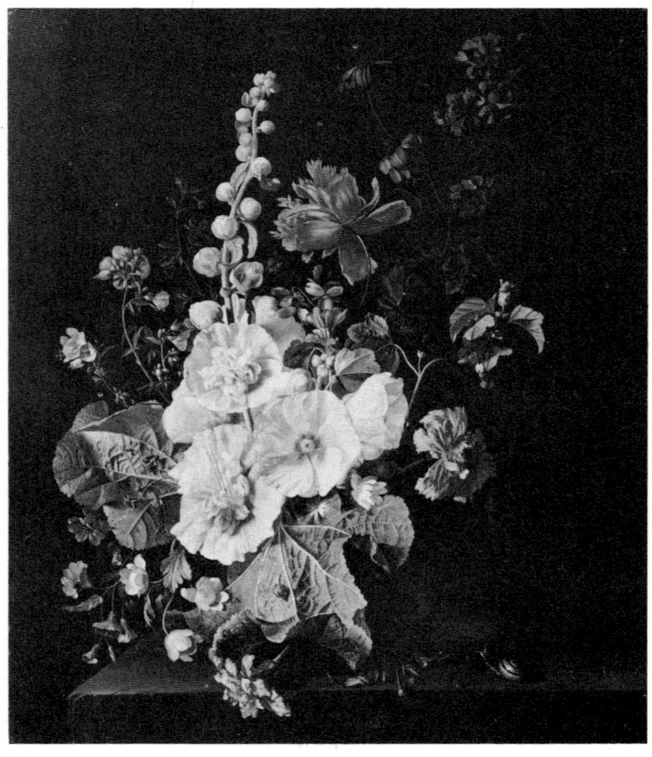

"Vase with Flowers" by Van Huyson

Reproduced by courtesy of the Trustees, The National Gallery, London

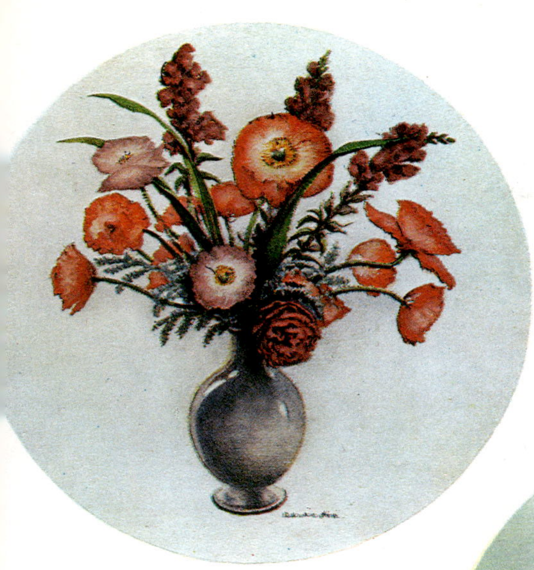

POPPIES

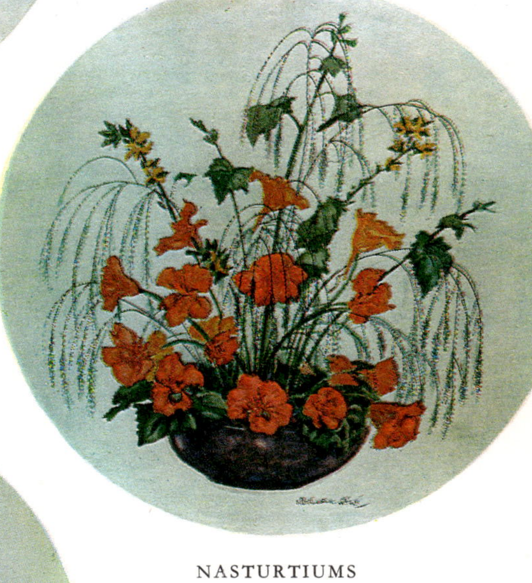

NASTURTIUMS

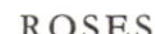

ROSES

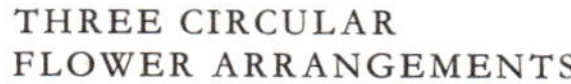

THREE CIRCULAR
FLOWER ARRANGEMENTS

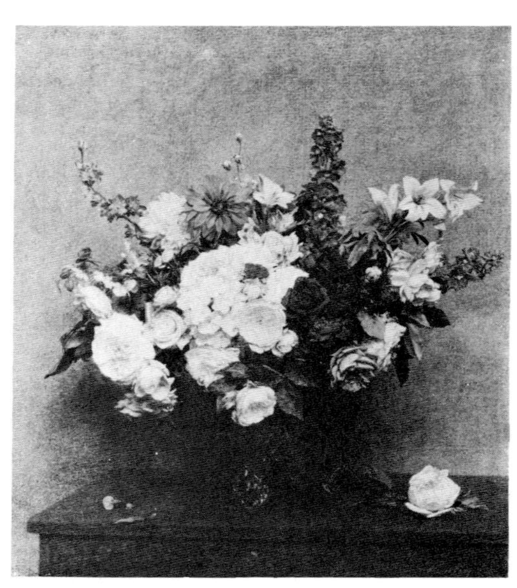

"Study of Flowers"
by
Fantin-la-Tour

Reproduced by courtesy of the Trustees, The National Gallery, London

skill and with a fascinating regard for minute detail, they are always lit with a certain eye for dramatic effect and further enhanced by the contrast provided by a dark, almost black, background.

In contrast to this abundance of material, Fantin-la-Tour, the great French flower painter, was content with Roses, Larkspur and Dahlias for his arrangement in a glass vase "Study of Flowers" (National Gallery), although I must not overlook the one golden Rose that lies on the table beside the vase! (I wonder whether this disregarded or loose flower was the original device, so assiduously and tiresomely followed by so many amateur painters in past years?)

Roses, I often think, were Fantin-la-Tour's chief love, and nobody surely has painted them better. See for yourself in the National Gallery, where he has two masterpieces. For in these examples we are captivated by their realness, within the terms of artistic reference, while all danger of sentiment is avoided. Indeed, we are beguiled by the pictorial integrity of the Rose rather than bewitched by any sentimental association connected with it.

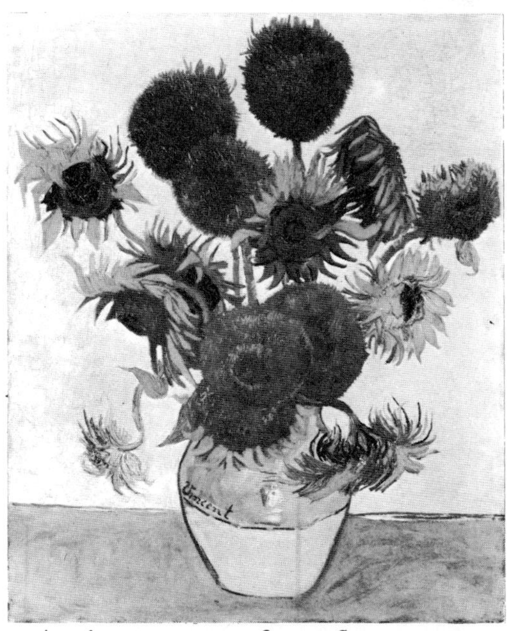

"Sunflowers" by Van Gogh

Reproduced by courtesy of the Trustees, The National Gallery, London

As time went on, fewer flowers seem to have been used and those of one species are often favoured. Well-known examples come from the hand of Manet who can concentrate and hold our attention on a couple of Rose-buds in a glass jam-jar, and Van Gogh, who lavishes all his love and passion on a few homely Sunflowers. It has been said that Renoir painted women like flowers and flowers like women. One knows what is meant by this poetic analogy and examples from his brush bear witness to the feminine grace he bestows on his simple flower pieces.

Certainly he and others achieved a dewy freshness and fragrance and what might be described as a "crushableness" in his paintings that has rarely been equalled. It was Cézanne, however, who almost fearful of sentiment, recaptured the solid form of flowers and in order to accomplish this, it is interesting to recall that, being a very slow worker, he is said to have had recourse to painting from artificial flowers, which do not fade or need replenishing! (It is not necessary I would hasten to add to emulate such a questionable policy, despite the fact that artificial flowers have improved out of all knowledge, sad to relate!)

Both Gauguin and Van Gogh took up the challenge of the

unsentimental or more robust rendering of flowers and produced paintings which could be said to have a botanical life of their own (which can also be said of some modern flower paintings!).

In these days when there is no dearth of flower models, it is interesting to recall that in the fourteenth, fifteenth and sixteenth centuries (as Sacheverell Sitwell reminds us) the number and variety of flowers at the painter's disposal was limited to "a very few Roses, and the simple stock-in-trade of Carnation and Pink, Daisies, Violets, Periwinkle, Poppies and Primroses. Such were their flowers."

In this brief review it is only necessary to add that whether the flower paintings are formal, exotic, romantic or strictly literal, it is clearly manifest that flowers of all kinds, shapes and colours, have inspired painters of all schools and all ages down to the present

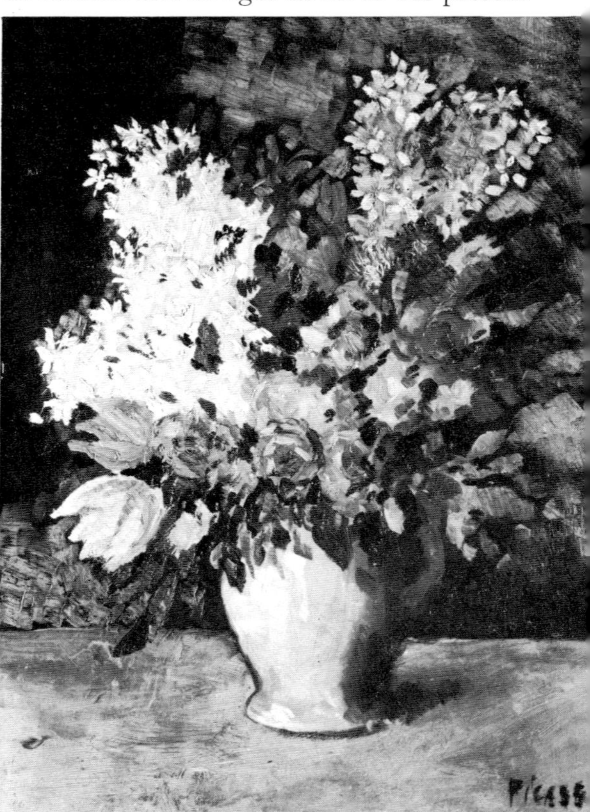

"Flowers in a Vase"
by Picasso

Reproduced by courtesy of the Trustees, The National Gallery, London day and to such varied artists as Bonnard, Matthew Smith, David Jones, Ivon Hitchens, Marcella Smith, John Farleigh, John Lancaster and even Picasso, whose well known "Flowers in a Vase" is, I believe, a most popular print.

It should be pointed out that of the great watercolour paintings of the past there are unfortunately fewer examples to be seen in our public art galleries. The reason is that in this medium, flower painting was relegated to the realms of botanical illustration and left largely in the hands of the accomplished amateur, thus remaining more or less unrecognized (except by the serious collectors) and thought undeserving of public patronage and display.

It is rather in private collections and in the Natural History Museum, Victoria and Albert and British Museums and in the Royal Botanic Gardens at Kew where you will be most likely to see examples from the hands of such famous painters as Van der Goes (fifteenth century), Alexander Marchall (seventeenth century), P. J. Redoute (eighteenth century), Clara Pope (nineteenth century) and Paul Robert (twentieth century).

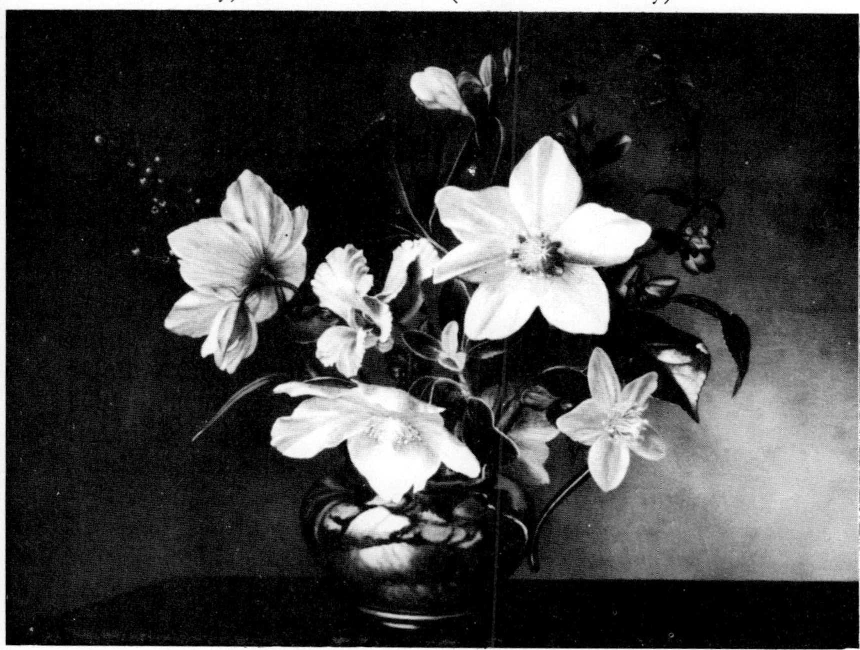

"Flower Piece" by John Lancaster

In the possession of J. B. Middleton, Charlestown, S. Carolina, U.S.A.

2: FLOWER APPRECIATION

There are some flowers which by tradition or legendary association have a festive, seasonal or romantic appeal.

The Madonna Lily is a typical example with its Easter message of immortality. In much the same way, but with opposite connotations, the Poppy has for years prompted more sombre reflections of the First World War. And while the Rose will always stir memories for the historian and the heart of young lovers, the Orchid's character might best be described by the story of the atheist who after having seen examples of it in the orchid exhibition at a flower show came away believing in the Devil!

Again, if such hardy (if diminutive) flowers as the Snowdrop, Primrose and Lily of the Valley, still continue to suffer from overtones of tender sentiment, the Tulip which modern painters have wrested (or rescued?) from the Flemish Old Masters, to fashion for their own ends, has taken very kindly to this pictorial 'face-lift'. Shrinking from any such modern grooming on the other hand, certain country yokels as the Foxglove, Bluebell and Campion can be mentioned as flowers who still appear ill-at-ease in the company of such fashionable cultivated dandies as the Lupin, Dahlia and Gladioli. (Indeed we can go merrily on listing flowers under their own special symbolic headings of legend, class or background!)

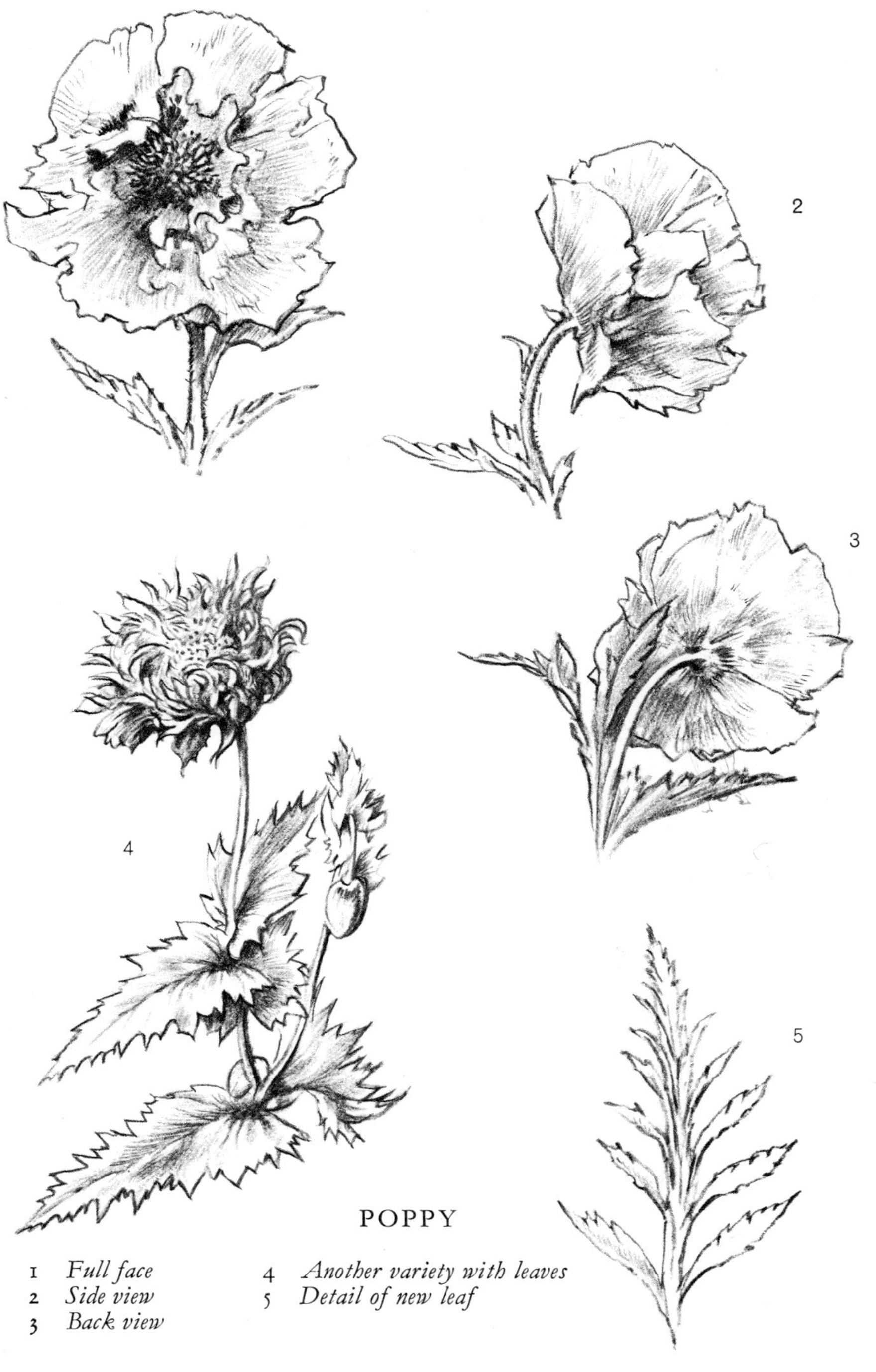

POPPY

1 *Full face*
2 *Side view*
3 *Back view*
4 *Another variety with leaves*
5 *Detail of new leaf*

TULIP

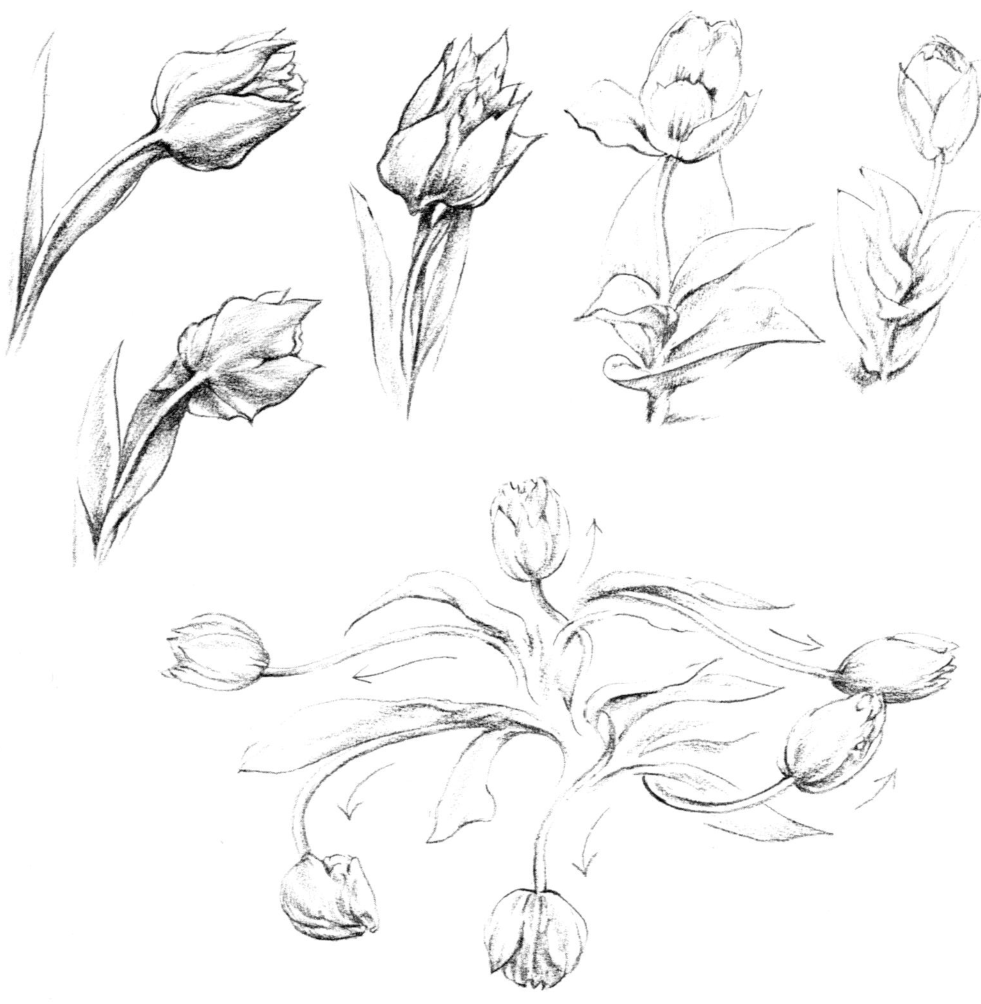

Details of various positions of flower and characteristic sinuous curves in growth

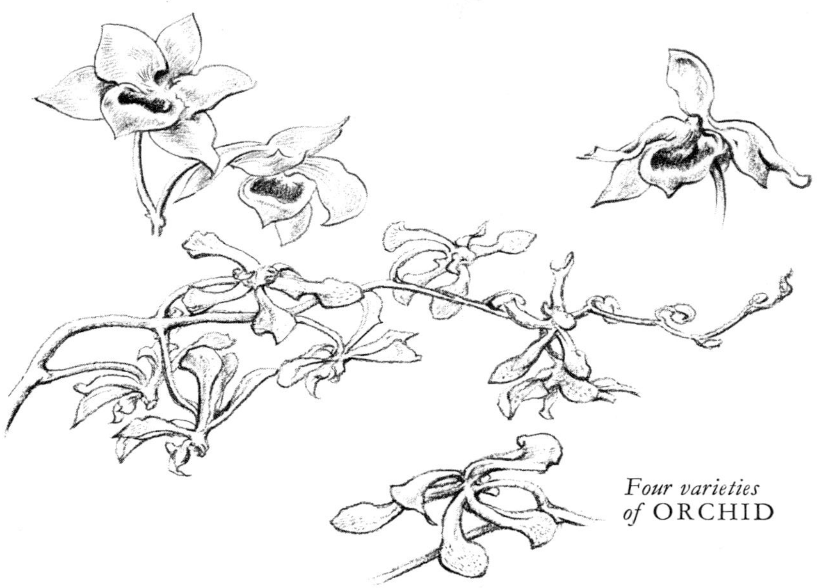

Four varieties of ORCHID

In addition to those mentioned, other flowers of the countryside that endear themselves to us by recollection of childhood and through the channels of poetry might well be given here as, according to season, they can in their turn be arranged harmoniously into successful flower paintings in watercolour or oil medium. Amongst others, special mention should be made of Cornflowers, Wild Daffodils, Honeysuckle, Tansy, Corn Marigolds, Wild Iris, Dog-rose, Pennywort, Bastard Balin, Ox-eyed Daisies, Purple Orchids, Hawthorn, Lords and Ladies, Fritillaries, Cowslips, Kingcups, Periwinkles, Reedmace and Meadow Saffron.

And, touching on names, as Clair Leighton reminds us in her engaging book *Four Hedges*, illustrated with the author's admirable engravings, "One feels even more strongly the pity of it that the old fashioned names of our flowers are fast being buried under the Latin titles. Hardly a soul now talks of his snapdragons, yet how much more beautiful that name is than antirrhinum? Pinks have become dianthus and in cottage gardens the humble marigold is transformed into calendula. And what of the cuckoopints? Was any flower the possessor of so many names, Priests Pintle, Lords and Ladies, Wild Arum and even Good King Henry!"

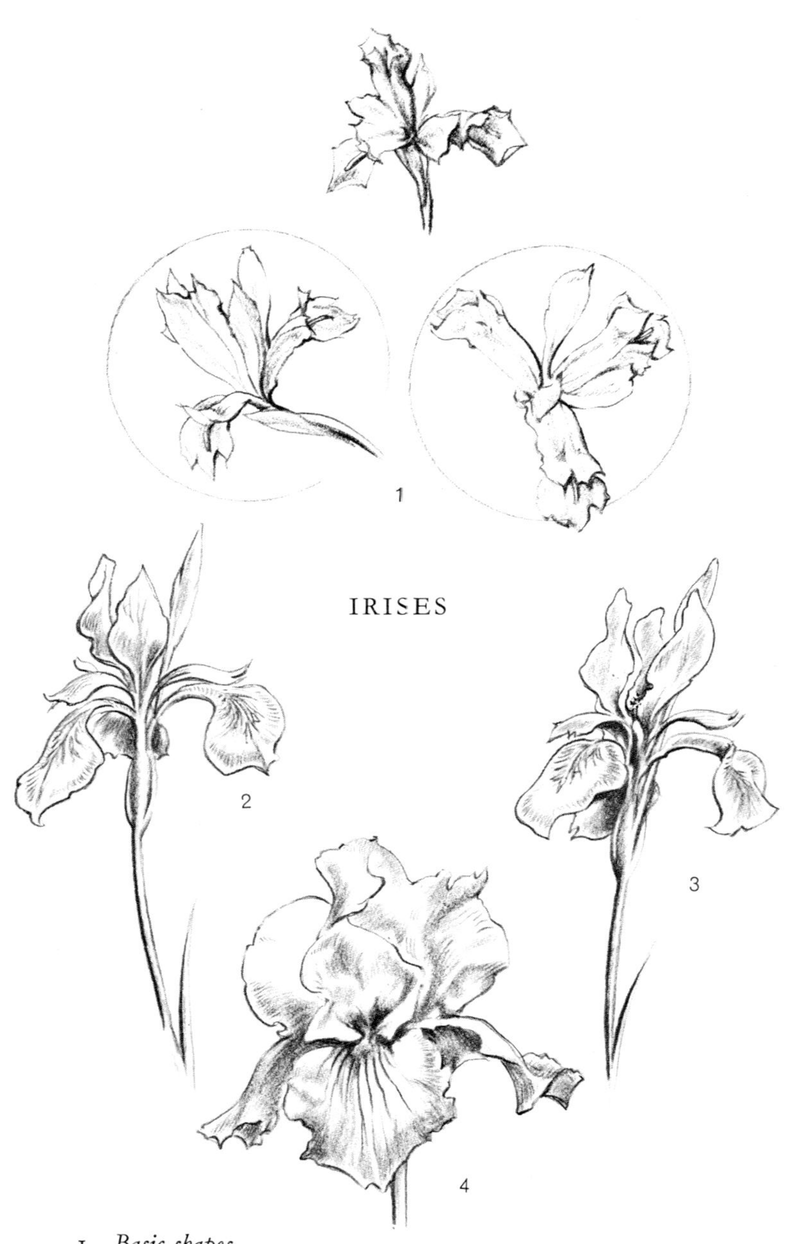

1 *Basic shapes*
2 and 3 *Subtle movement observed while drawing a single bloom*
4 *Water iris*

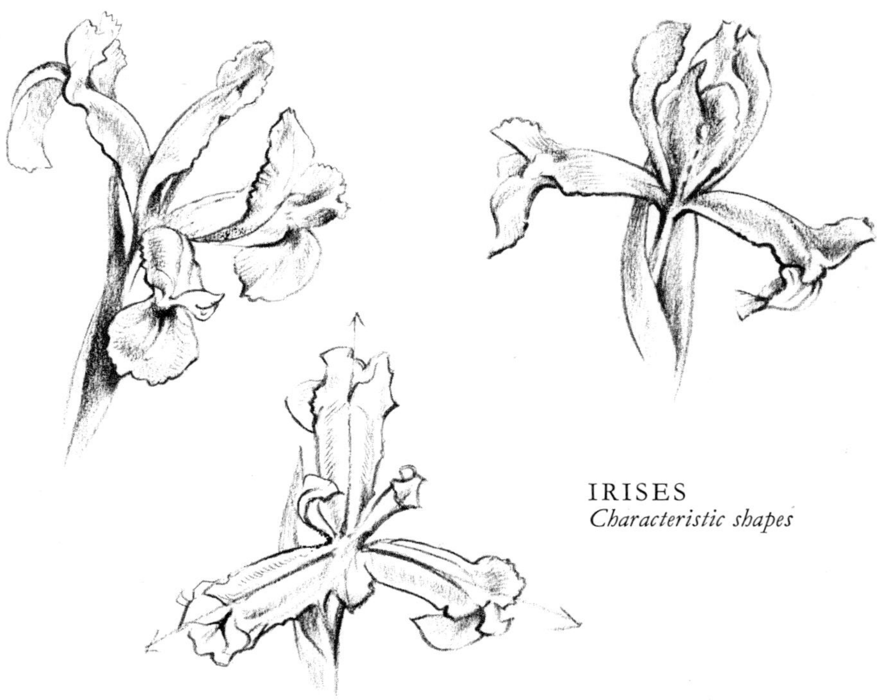

IRISES
Characteristic shapes

And who could resist the Lincolnshire name for the wild pansy: Meet-her-in-the-entry, Kiss-her-in-the-buttery, or Jack-by-the-Hedge and Venus's looking-glass?

By mentioning these by name I hope the reader will be encouraged to enlarge his range of wild flowers, for in the end, of course, it is only by trial-and-error that we learn to discriminate and make our final choice amongst so many tempting floral wares at the painter's disposal.

Of the garden and shop variety, I have appended a list at the end of this book, and although I have perforce to include the Daffodil (which gladdens the heart and dazzles the eye with its promise of spring), by the very nature of its vivid yellow colour it still proves, in my experience, an awkward guest when introduced for painting purposes into the mixed company of other flowers but, I must add, a tantalizing flower to draw!

3: FLOWER DRAWING

Flower paintings, as Wilfrid Blunt points out with wit, "have been made at different times by diverse types of artists and for diverse purposes, by bold explorers in the cause of science, and by timid spinsters to the Glory of God"! We have benefited from the former and all suffered from the latter, chiefly I believe because of the over-sentimental approach and latent feebleness, mistaken for delicacy, of drawing.

At the risk of repeating a truism we must really *study* flowers if we wish to paint them well. In this context "Consider the Lilies . . . *how* they grow" is very apposite to the beginner. To consider any flower, for that matter, we should sit down and *draw* it. It is only then that we really find out all about it. Its shape, its form, its distinctive personality and its way of growth. And this knowledge is only vouchsafed by drawing the flower, not only side-view but full-face, three-quarter, back view and in short—all round! And how different these various aspects are found to be and how useful the knowledge when painting a flower piece where some blooms face us—others of the same species perhaps offer us their profiles and others again turn their faces, if not their backs, on us!

For, contrary to expectation, it is only fair to the reader to emphasize that flowers do not make docile sitters!

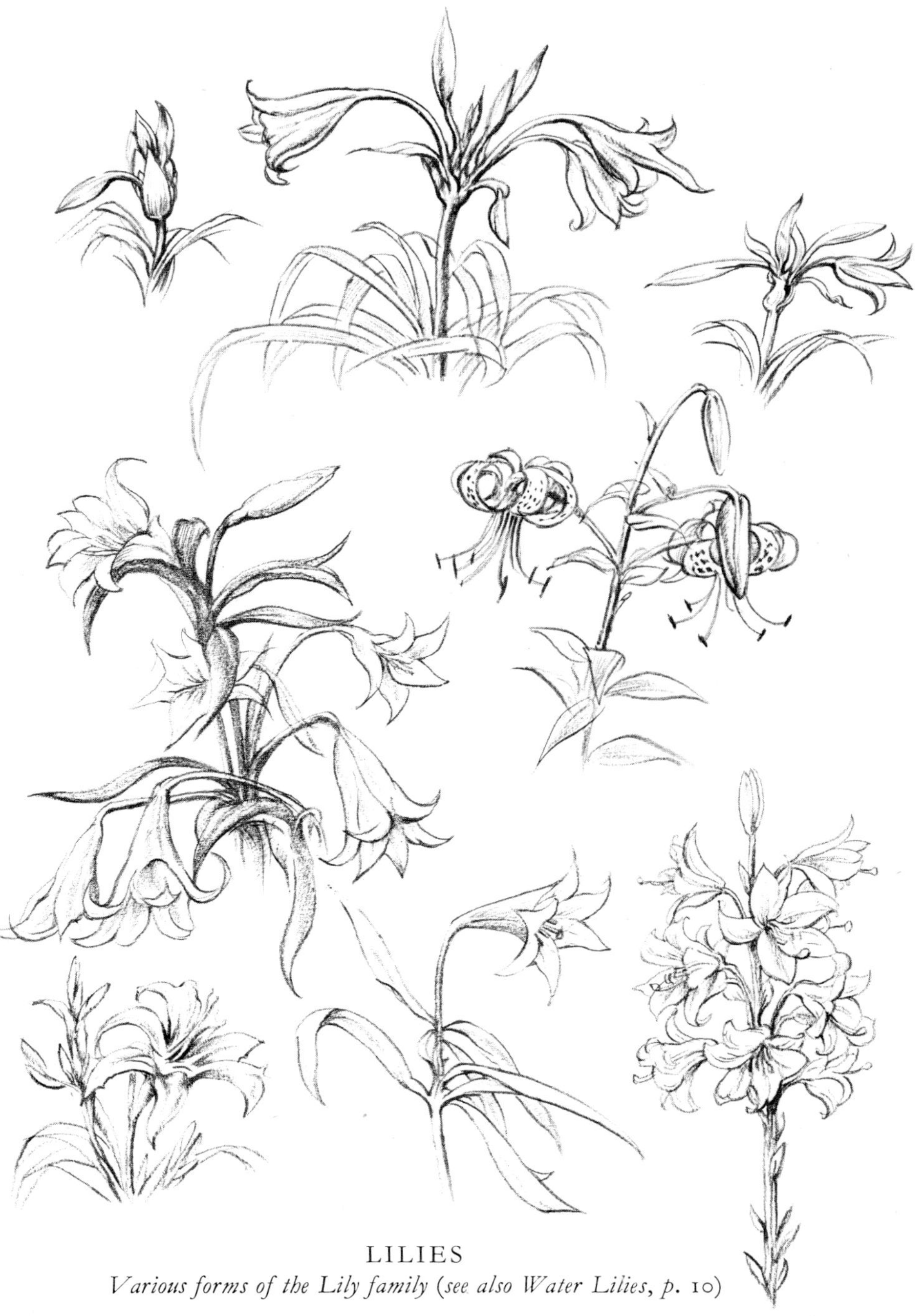

LILIES

Various forms of the Lily family (*see also Water Lilies*, *p.* 10)

Any breeze, however slight, will set the flower quivering and trembling on its stalk, and that is only to be expected when it is growing wild or in the garden, but in the calm of a studio, flower stalks curve or straighten themselves, and petals will magically open or close even going to the length of turning their faces from us to the light, and this can be very disconcerting.

Viewed in this aspect, when the individual flower shapes and colours are painted as units in a carefully planned composition, such perversity presents a real problem which only hard study can overcome.

It has rightly been said "Facility in colouring is easily acquired —but a correct eye for drawing is only to be rendered by constant observation". And this scrutiny and study should become our pleasure and not a task, for in the very nature of our subject, flowers can make such lovely drawings and are in many ways more diverse in shape, size and coloration than any of Nature's living properties. Nature moreover ordains that all her forms, details and additions are always in perfect accord with one another. Thus the study of the leaves which accompany flowers should evoke our admiration for their fitness of purpose. The foliage is always right for the particular flower and supports or shows it off to the best advantage. Look at the lance-like polished sheath of the Tulip, and the spiky fringed leaf of the Lupin. Compare the simple shape and small size of the Rose leaf with the wide feathery spread of the Delphinium foliage and imagine if these leaves were exchanged one with another!

It certainly helps if the initial task of drawing flowers correctly is rewarded by drawing them well and with ease, for it must be admitted that clumsily drawn flowers which are the outcome of obvious labour, despite care of arrangement and beauty of colour, will fail to satisfy the discriminating critic. For all flowers, although they may not have an equal appeal, possess a grace, a personality, a distinctive quality of design and pattern as well as colour which should be studied and emulated with loving care.

When drawing the flower therefore, it is important whenever

DAHLIAS

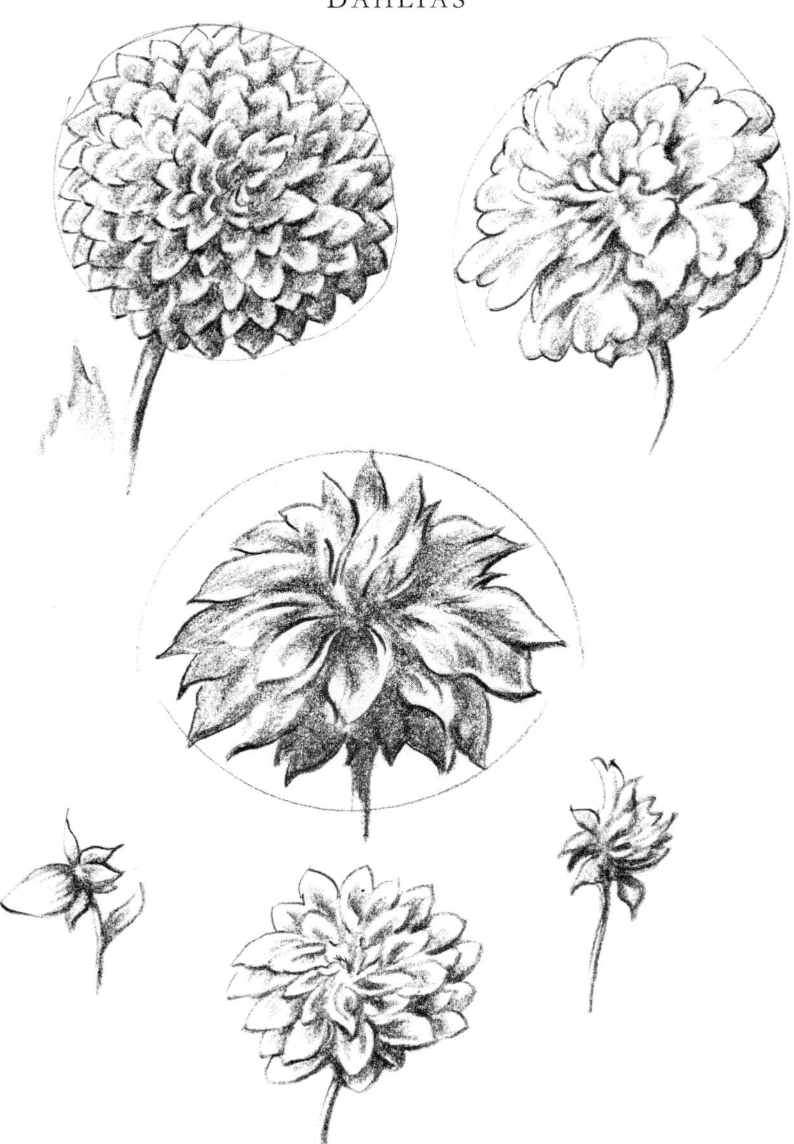

Characteristic circular shape of growth of DAHLIAS . . .

possible to include the leaf and note its size in comparison with the flower and its distinctive way of growth. Walter Hood Fitch suggests with, I think, some reason, that "a knowledge of botany, however slight (and that is the operative word for us), is of great value in enabling the artist to avoid errors which are occasionally perpetuated in respectable drawings, such as introducing an abnormal number of stamens in a flower; giving it an inferior ovary when it should have a superior one and vice versa . . . for a little knowledge would enable them to be avoided". And, he adds, "it is more creditable that one's works should furnish an example than a warning". A nice touch.

Thus, in a straight stem there is always some degree of curve,

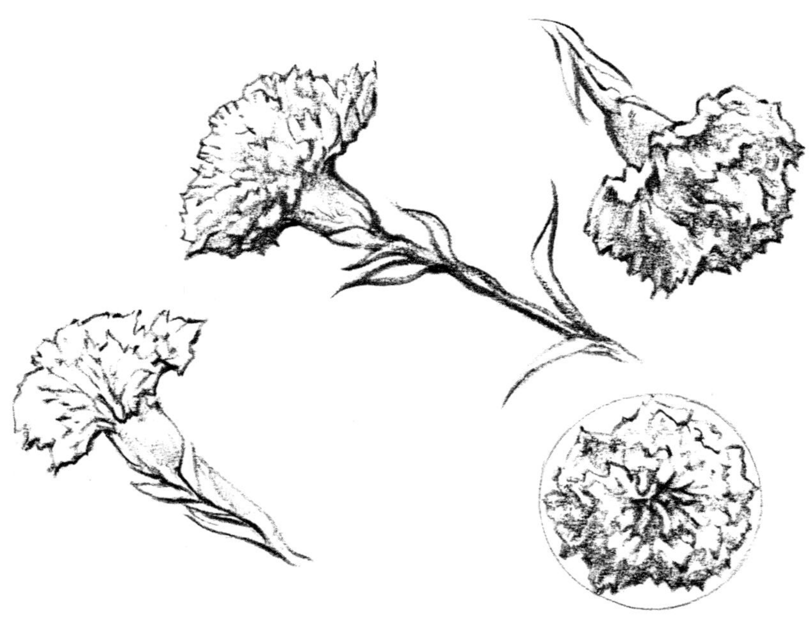

. . . *and some aspects of* CARNATIONS

and note that the stem is either square, round, ringed, etc. In drawing leaves, it is better to draw in the midrib *first*, noting that it should always have some degree of curve, and mark *where* the veins sprang from.

It should also be noticed that leaves are either "simple" in outline, serrated, pinnated or lobed, and that they have a habit of turning over at the tip. With flowers a simple example to start with is a Primrose. More complicated shapes are the Iris, the Nasturtium, the *Aconitum* and the Fuchsia. Those that are termed labiate are often varied in form and the tube may be longer than the calyx and the upper lip shorter or longer than the lower one. Of all flowers, perhaps the Orchid is the most difficult to draw correctly, being so varied in shape, size and form and colour! The details alone confuse the eye, composed of a germen or ovary, surmounted by three sepals, two petals, a lip and a column.

When we consider the number and variety of flowers at the painter's disposal, there is no danger of a dearth of models, despite the fact that they are not all easily accessible nor indeed are they all equally attractive for drawing or painting purposes. But it must not be forgotten when at a loss for drawing material that wild flowers, as I have already mentioned, are equally *drawable* and readily conform to floral arrangements and should not be excluded from our gallery of flower studies. To illustrate this chapter I have given, I hope, enough examples of flower details to whet the reader's appetite to follow up his own collection of flower studies.

For these drawings, most artists, I believe, use lead pencil and a fairly hard one at that. As it happens I still prefer a carbon (B or BB) to lead, as it gives a crisper line and unlike plumbago, is not prone to become shiny when deep tone is used. Charcoal, although admittedly more sensitive and suggestive than either, lacks the essential precision of a point and even when fixed, does not take kindly to washes of colour and in many such studies of separate flowers, transparent washes of colour are desirable and give an added quality which in botanical drawing especially is often employed with charming results.

The use of coloured pencils is another attractive method by which the actual black-and-white drawing can be further enhanced. Their wide range of colours will be found all-sufficient for a close approximation of the original tint.

It is well to fix the initial drawing before working over it with the coloured pencils, otherwise they will pick up the lead or carbon lines and darken the colour.

No elaborate background colours should be attempted and if only a flat tint is desired, then tinted paper is recommended as many shades are obtainable in artists' colourmen shops, and you

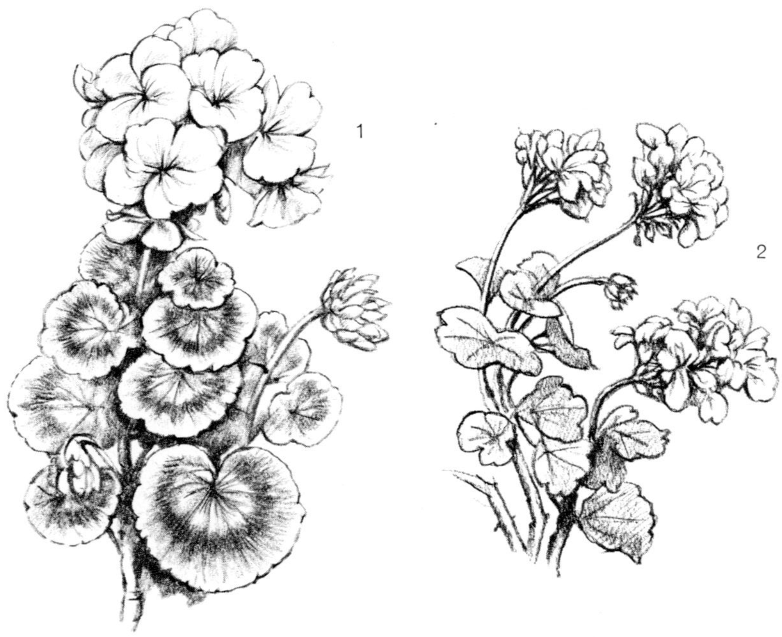

GERANIUM

1 *Flowers and leaves, full face*

2 *Side view, showing attachment of flowers and leaves on stem*

HYDRANGEA
Small single blooms growing in mass

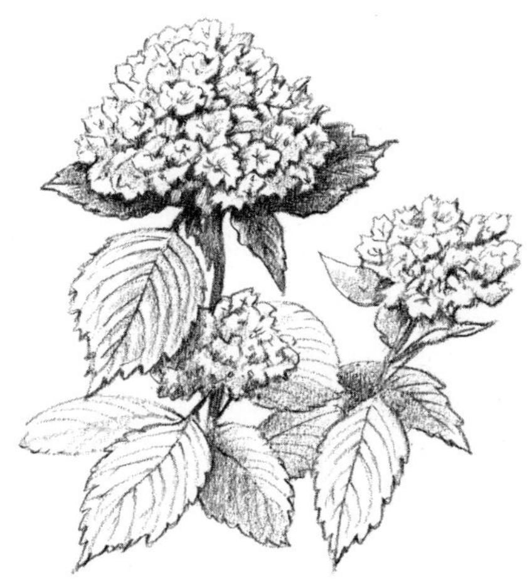

can choose the shade which will harmonize with the colour scheme of the flowers.

If indeed the first consideration of a successful flower painting is in making studies of individual blossoms by which one is free to concentrate on their characteristics, then what might be thought of as a laborious task will surely prove a rewarding pleasure. But to those of my readers who flinch from such an exacting exercise and who in turn regard, and with suspicion, all flower paintings as being the outcome of such laboured inspection, I would encourage the very opposite approach! I would advise a carefree attack with a loaded brush and no preliminary drawing, motivated only by an intense desire to render the impact of flowers as something living—in short "to brighten up the home"! And if I venture to say further that if this is how you personally react to flowers, then that is the way you should *try* to paint them and have no conscience about the matter, a qualification or warning is necessary because in the urge to create a riot of colour, a sumptuous effect, a cavalcade of lustrous blooms, you may at first only achieve a floral firework display, blinding to the eye and well-nigh impossible to contemplate, by which I mean to live with. Let us then suppose that discretion curbs this impulse and something less emotional (or sentimental) is attempted, at least to begin with!

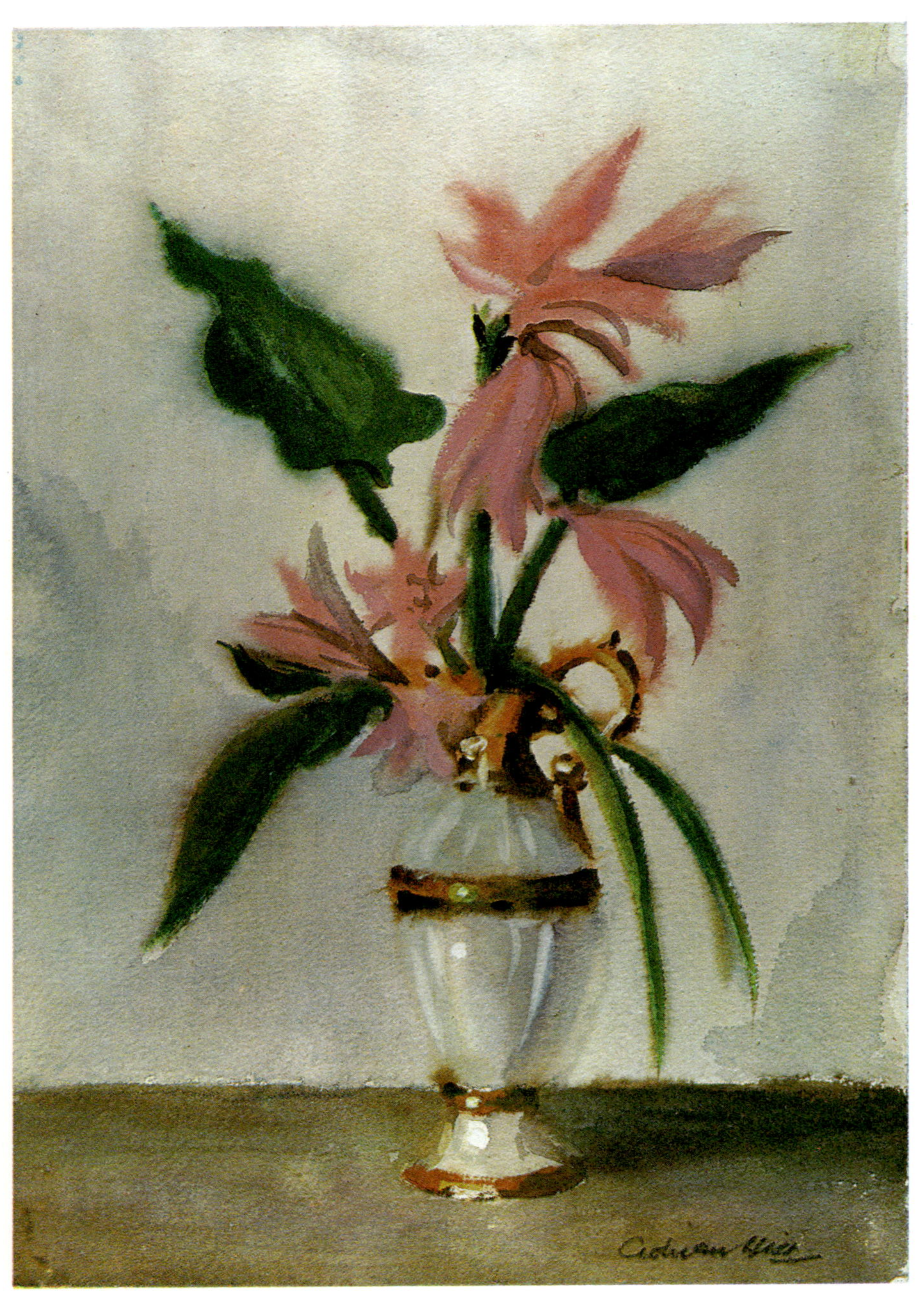

LILIES IN A JUG

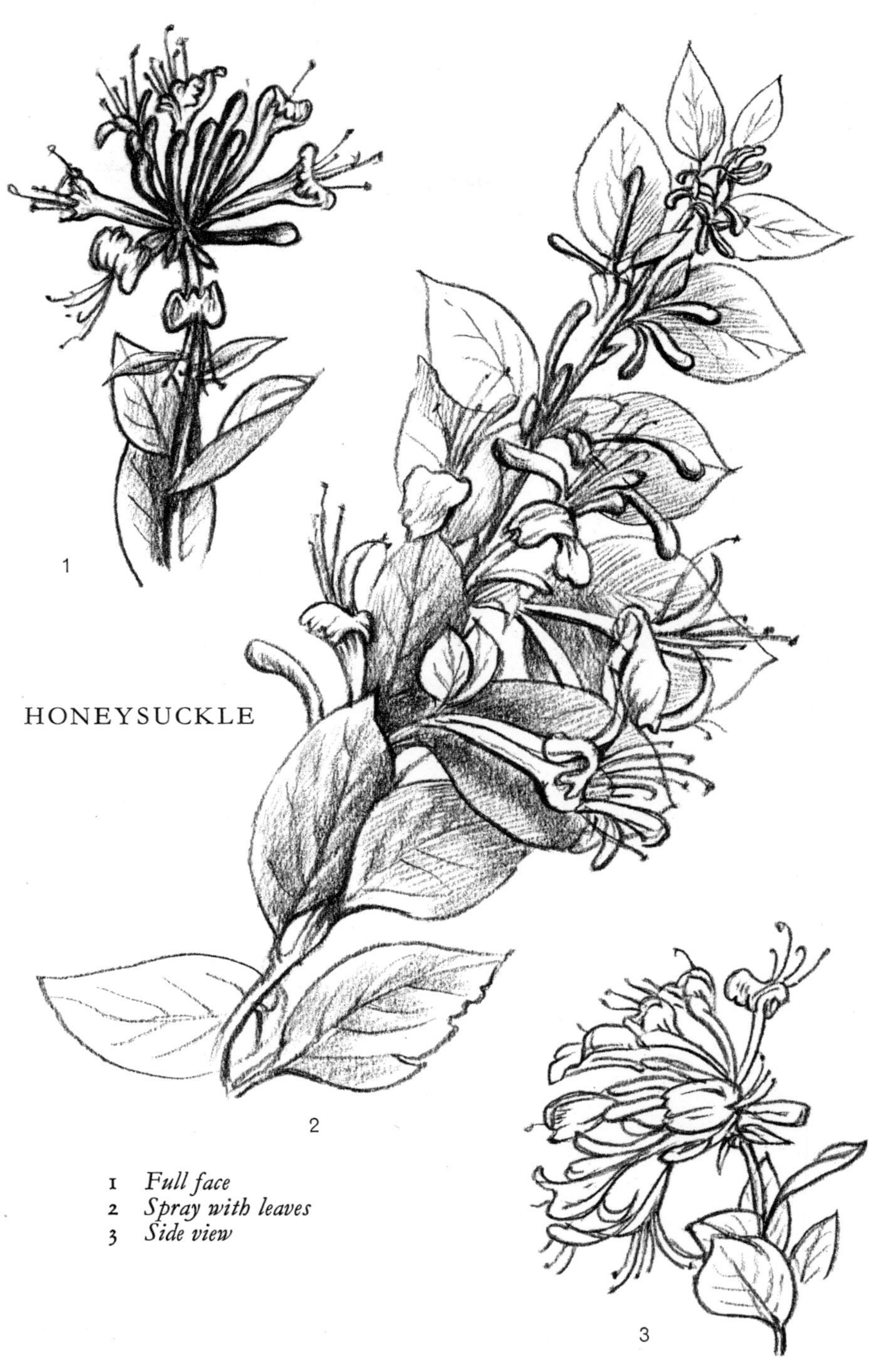

1 *Full face*
2 *Spray with leaves*
3 *Side view*

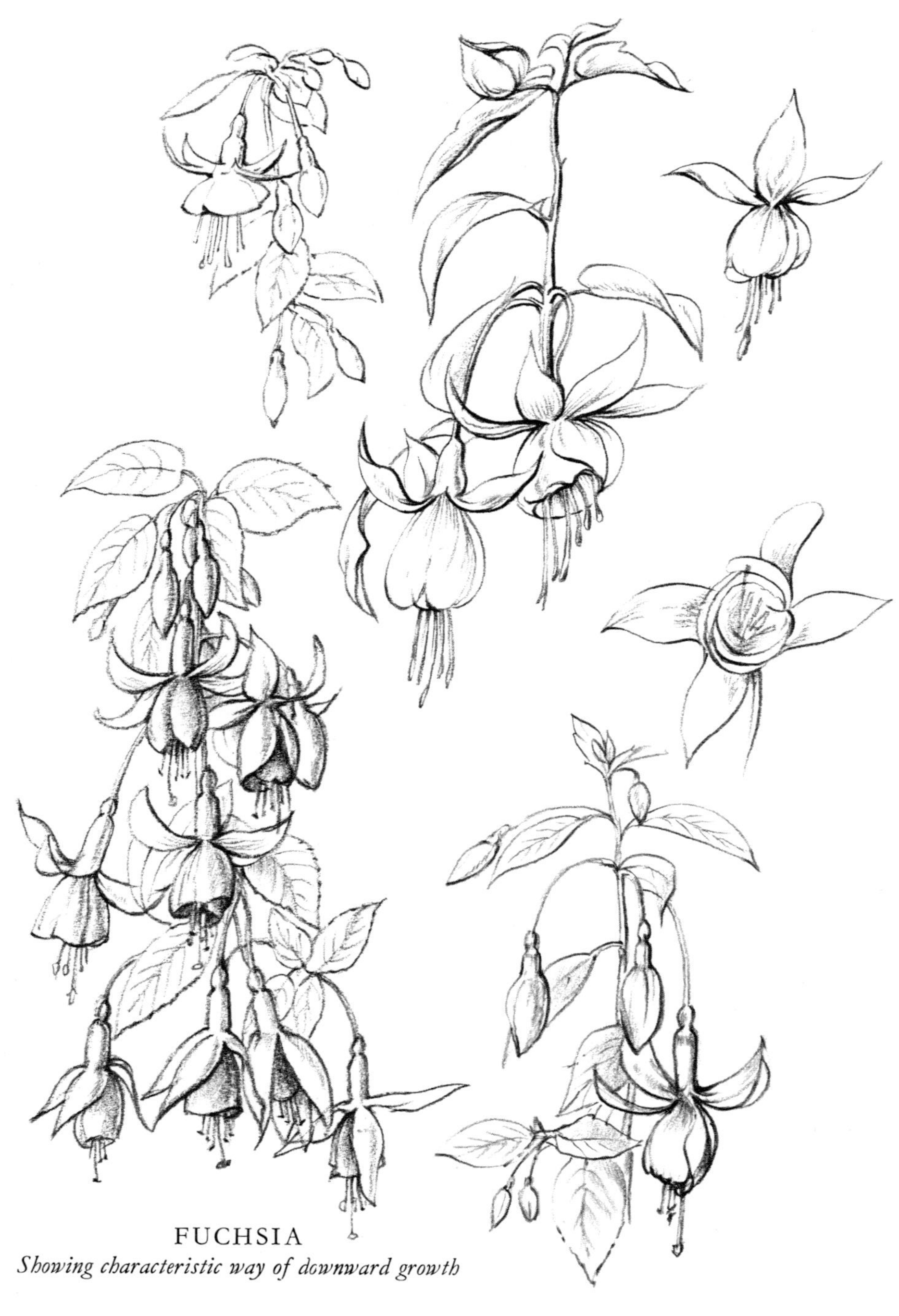

FUCHSIA

Showing characteristic way of downward growth

4: THE WATERCOLOUR MEDIUM

For the representation of flowers many media and techniques have at one time or another been employed. If you asked half-a-dozen professional painters how they painted a flower piece they would in all probability disclose a variety of approaches, especially in technique and quite possibly at variance with one another. Each would develop his own style and medium and confess his particular penchant for certain flowers. This is inevitable and natural, otherwise all their paintings would have a deadly similarity. But as professionals, well qualified to do their job, they would all reveal one very important factor in common. Each would start off with a knowledge of composition and thus base his painting on an acceptable design. Apart then from advice on this medium any attempt to prescribe a foolproof method of procedure would cramp the student's desire to be himself. All one can hope to do is suggest a way, born out of the author's own experience, which will help the beginner to avoid the more obvious pitfalls which enthusiasm and eagerness to produce a finished painting so often overlook. It must be clearly understood, therefore, that the following chapters on flower painting in watercolour and oils are addressed to the beginner who desires some sound method which will *start* him on the right road until such time as he feels ready to determine his own future course of travel into the delectable

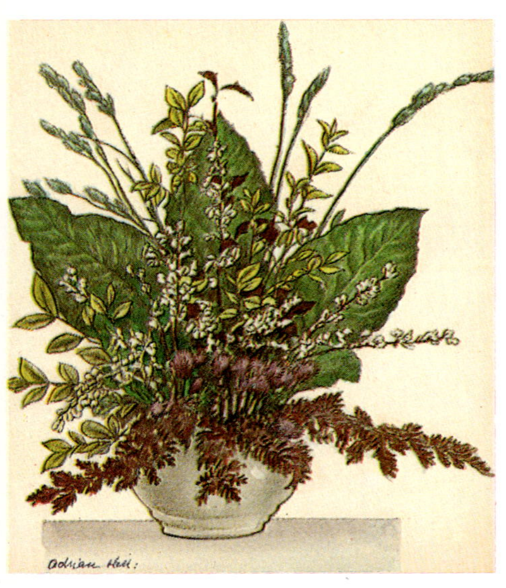

CHIVES, DOCK LEAVES AND GRASSES

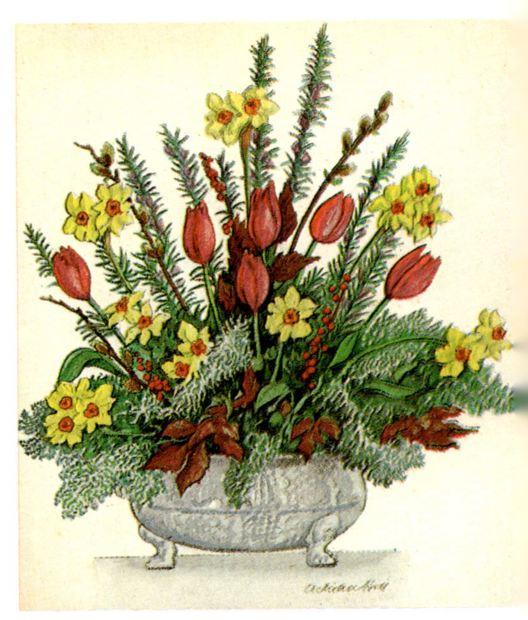

TULIPS AND NARCISSI

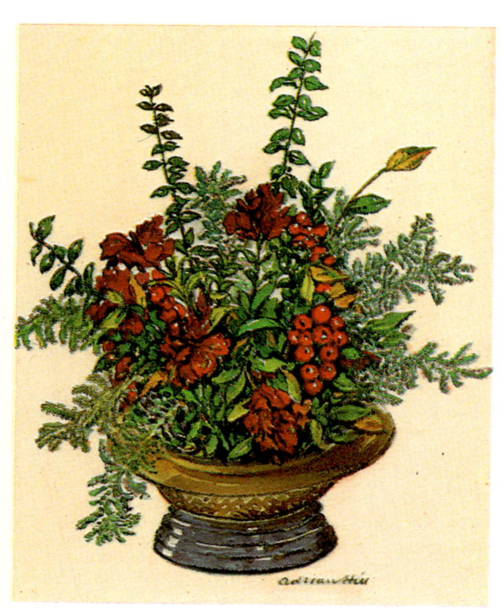

BERRIES AND FOLIAGE

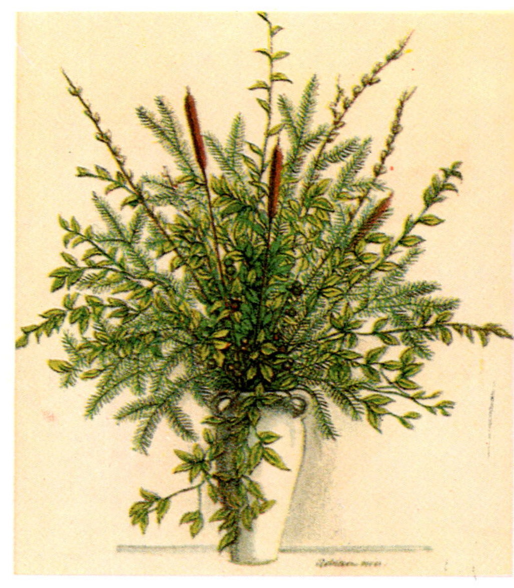

BULRUSHES, PRIVET AND YEW

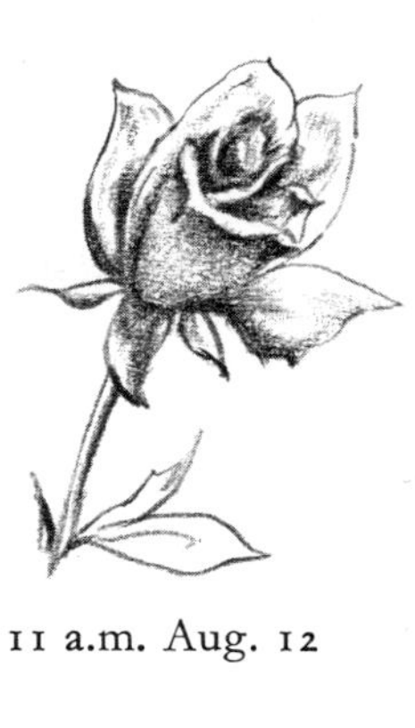

11 a.m. Aug. 12

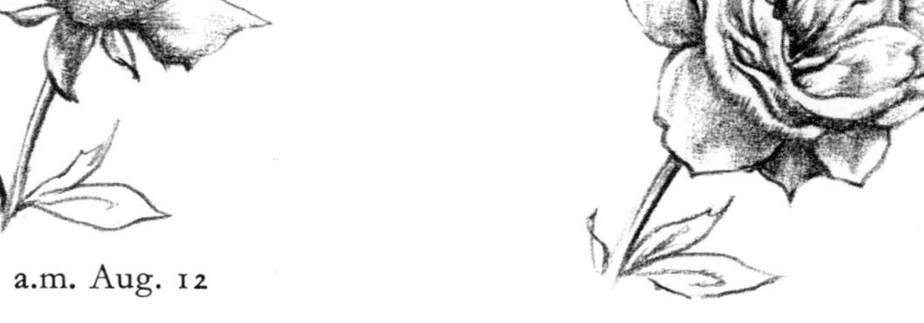

11 a.m. Aug. 13

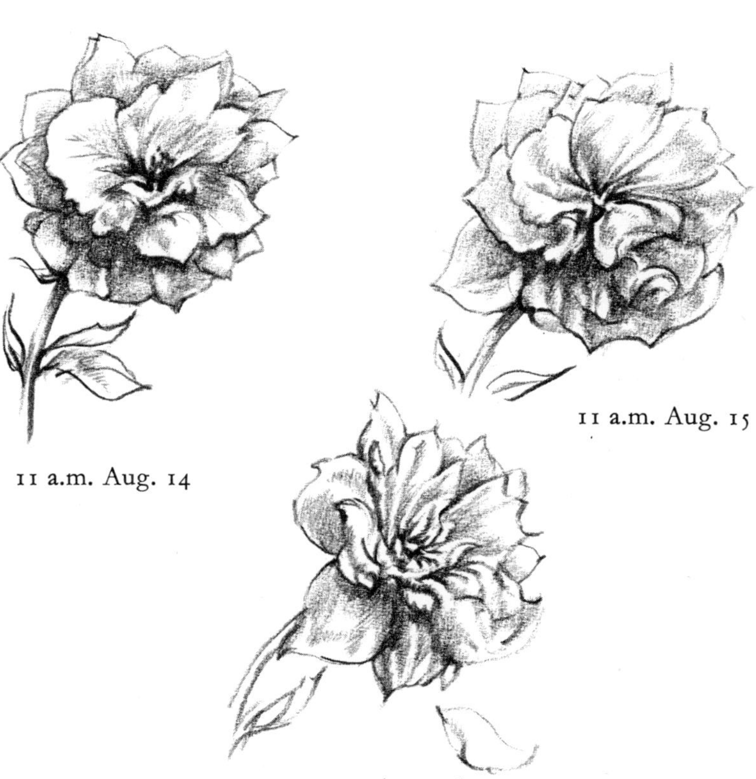

11 a.m. Aug. 15

11 a.m. Aug. 14

11 a.m. Aug. 16

Five days in the life of a Rose

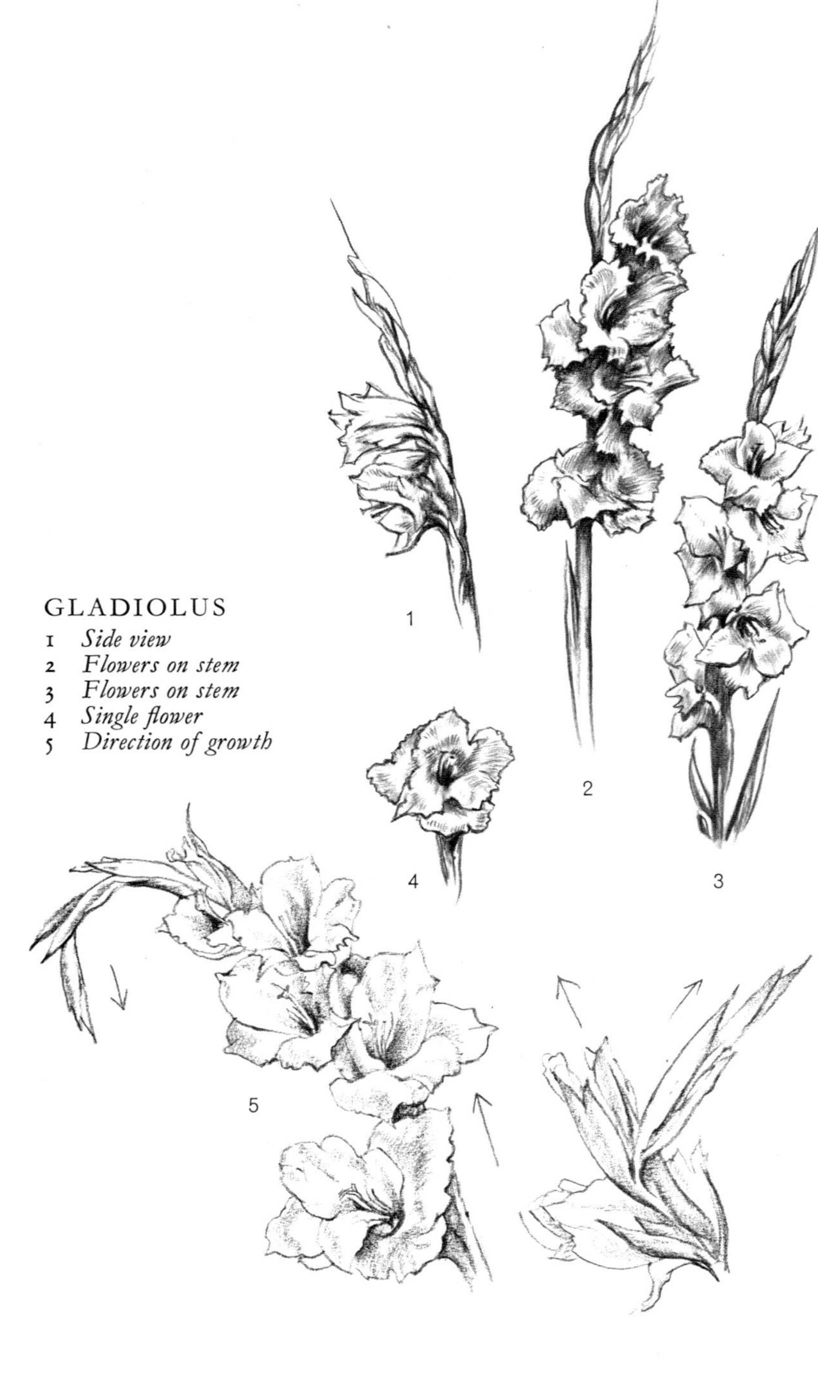

GLADIOLUS

1 *Side view*
2 *Flowers on stem*
3 *Flowers on stem*
4 *Single flower*
5 *Direction of growth*

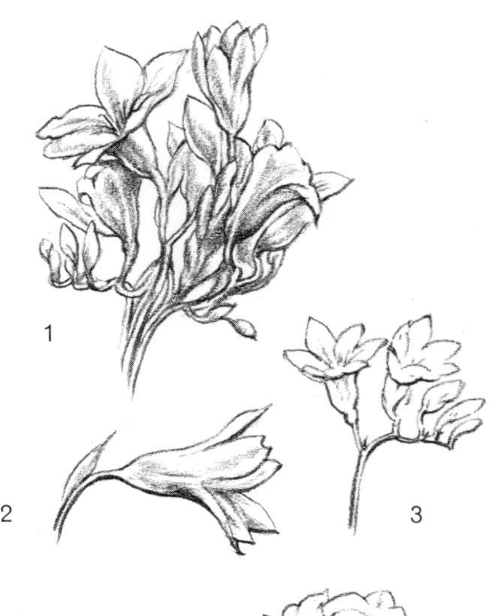

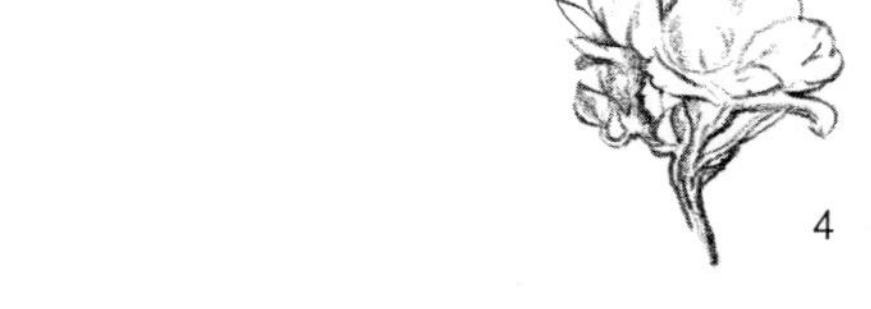

FREESIA
1 *Bunch formation*
2 *Single bloom, side view*
3 *Red Freesias*
4 *Double-flowered variety*

country of flowers, which holds out so many exciting bypaths to tempt him off the traditional beaten track.

One, perhaps for some the only, accepted and traditional method of procedure in painting a flower piece in watercolours is to begin with a slight—faint is more descriptive—pencil drawing, which is used only to establish by indication the planning and placing of the composition on the paper. This should define the "approximate" shape of the flowers (they constantly move) and establish the spaces between them, the stems, foliage and top of vase or bowl. Though no detail is employed or required, a hasty scaffolding will jeopardize a firm fundamental design and as all subsequent drawing is left to the painting brush, it is very important as I have mentioned before, to have had practice in drawing flowers, as absolute precision and delicacy in painting them is essential. The chief aim indeed is to avoid any evidence of

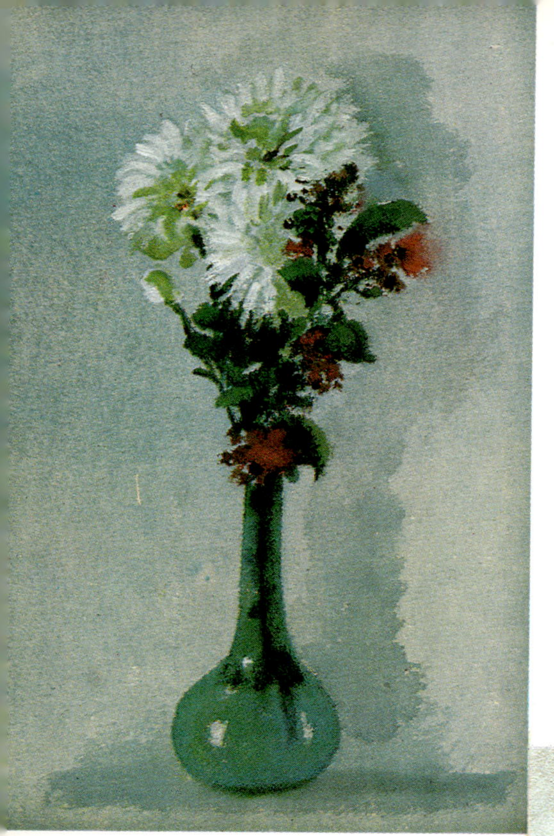

CHRYSANTHEMUMS
IN A GLASS BOTTLE

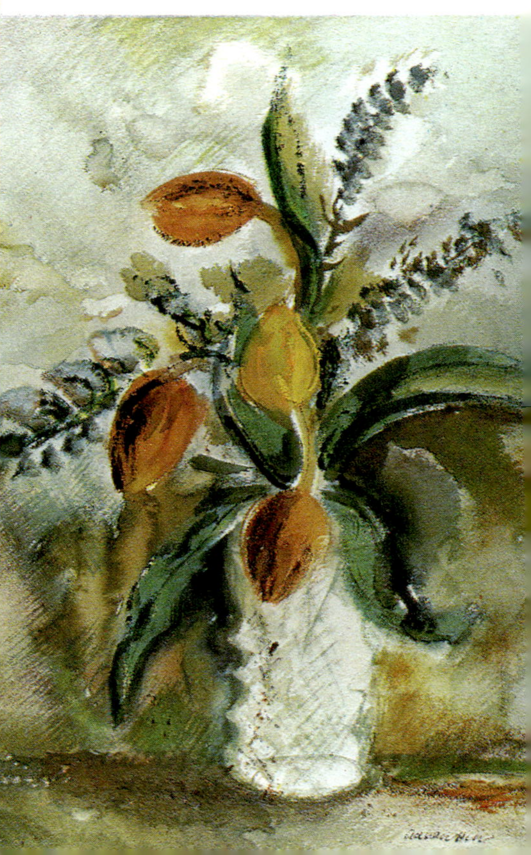

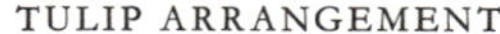

TULIP ARRANGEMENT

labour which is painfully obvious if alteration by over-painting has been found necessary. In this respect, then, mixing on the palette should be reduced to the minimum, for apart from the time factor, over-mixing will spoil the freshness and cloud the transparency of your colours. And to secure maximum clarity of tint, I recommend two containers of water so that your brush does not become stained with the subtle impurities of previous cleanings. It must be remembered that a certain loss of colour brilliance is in any case inevitable when drying out.

Tradition has laid it down that before the actual painting is begun, your paper should be moistened all over, so a good stout quality is advised if cockling of the surface is to be avoided. (Pasteless board will obviate all danger of this.) The advantage of working over a damp surface is that it will keep your handling broad and loose in treatment, and for this reason your initial washes should be applied at full strength in order to combat the additional moisture of the paper. This may sound difficult, but if the principle is accepted, practice will soon confirm the truth of it, which will be only too obvious if not followed, for there is nothing so unflower-like as a dry tight painting! All details of form, detail and accent should be left as late as possible, necessary as they are to emphasize the characteristics of the chosen blooms and such definitions—when we come to them—must not be overworked but applied with precision and the lightest of touches. It is only by such means that the right fusion will be achieved.

It will be realized only too soon that flowers are notoriously fugitive and prone to move with almost human perversity! "Only those who have attempted to draw flowers can appreciate what restless models these can be, how quickly petals open and stems curve."

As I have already warned the reader, however static flowers appear, they do in fact change position in a subtle manner, notably those that grow on longish stalks like Tulips and Daffodils, while Arum Lilies are notoriously susceptible to movement owing to their fleshy stalks. It should also be remembered that most flowers that grow on fleshy stalks, as distinct from those on woody stems, will always turn their heads to the light. Ignorance of these little points can make the beginner's task more difficult when, other things being equal, the job itself presents enough problems to engage the eye and hand!

Moreover the coloration of many flowers is so dazzling or subtle that when painting against time an approximation of the hue and tone is all one can hope for. Thus any slowing down to concentrate on what has been well described as "caressing the object" will only result in a painstaking painting.

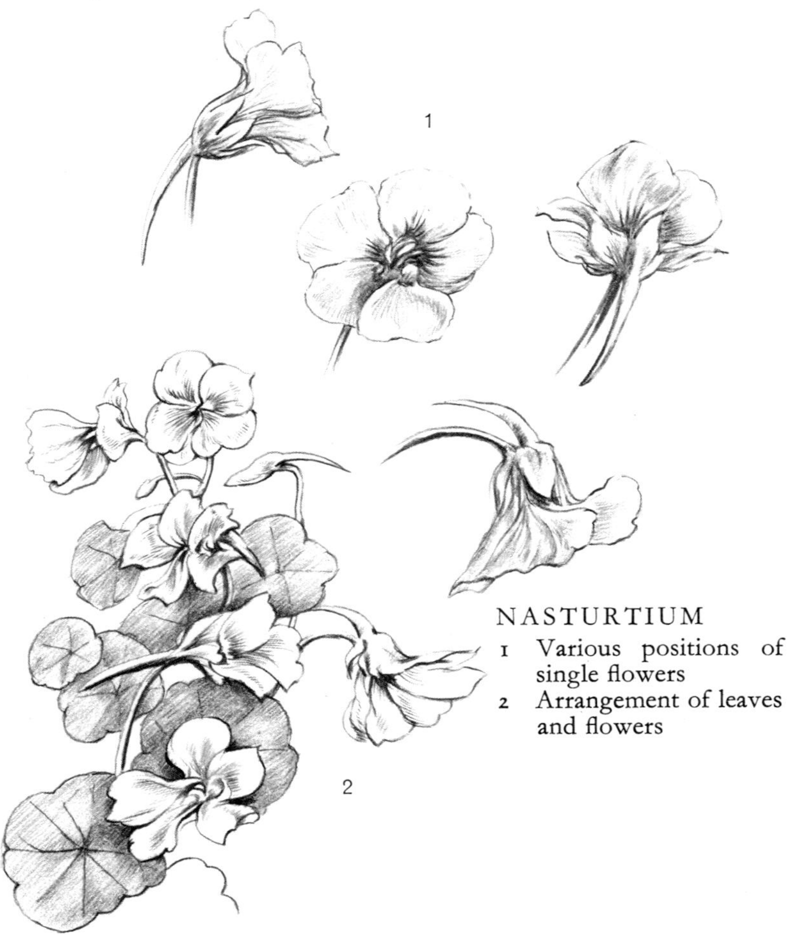

NASTURTIUM
1 Various positions of single flowers
2 Arrangement of leaves and flowers

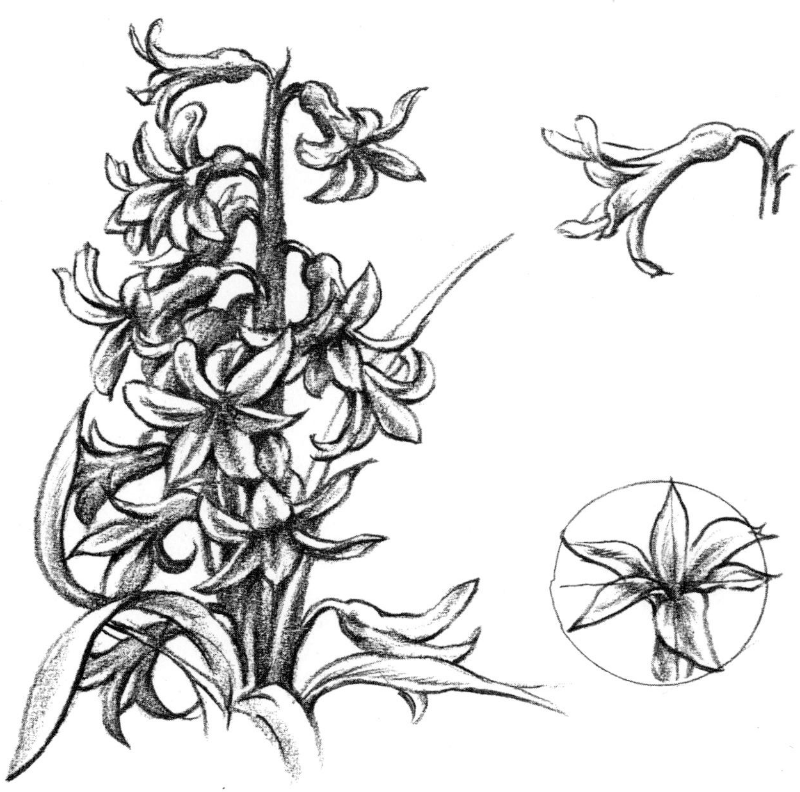

HYACINTH with details

The reader would be well advised to choose a plain lightish background comprising one or two tints introduced, rather than well mixed, and floated on all over the paper while it is still damp. This formula should never become a self-imposed rule, but in the early stages will serve its purpose of preventing the background from becoming too colourful and consequently "busy" in which case it is apt to come in front of your flowers.

Before this wash is quite dry and with a bigger brush than you may feel necessary, paint (or draw in your colour) the shape of your flowers, starting with those that form the outline of your design, so that the edges are soft against your background tint. This is to avoid a cut-out appearance of the flowers which is difficult to prevent if the background is dry or if you leave painting it in until you have completed the blooms themselves. Keep all foliage a warmer green than it may appear, and when leaves are in close contact with light or white flowers, strengthening or lowering the tint or tone will by comparison enhance the brilliance that is so difficult to achieve without the use of chinese white. (A purist in this medium is always loath to resort to opaque colours—but there are occasions when the means justify the end.)

With your painting so far completed, there comes that almost irresistible temptation to add some last detail, now apparent when you compare bit by bit your painting with the original. You only intend a touch or two, but, alas, it rarely stops there, and you find yourself involved in a general tidying up all over. Such mistaken finish must be resisted at all costs (as I know to my own cost in the early days). I have suggested this method of procedure, as *one way* by which the more obvious pitfalls can be avoided. There are, however, many questions still unanswered, to which only personal practice, study and experiment are able to furnish satisfactory replies. To many, and I must include myself in the number, a sensitive swift impression is often superior to a faithful and careful representation. Flower life is not dependent on labels nor freshness and poetry of flowers on conscientious classification (especially I should hasten to add in this particular technique and medium of watercolour *painting*). But obviously there will be some

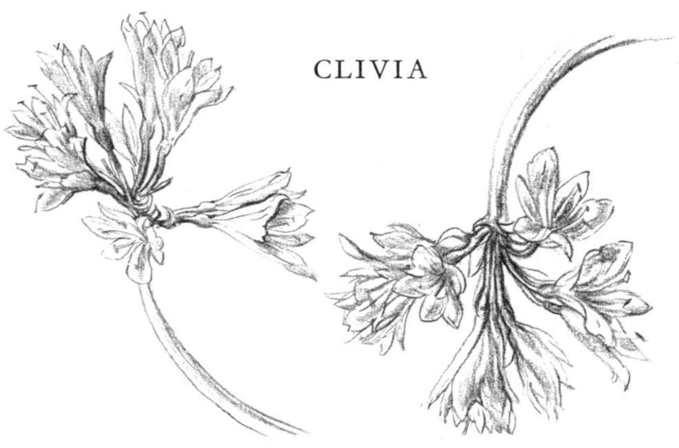
CLIVIA

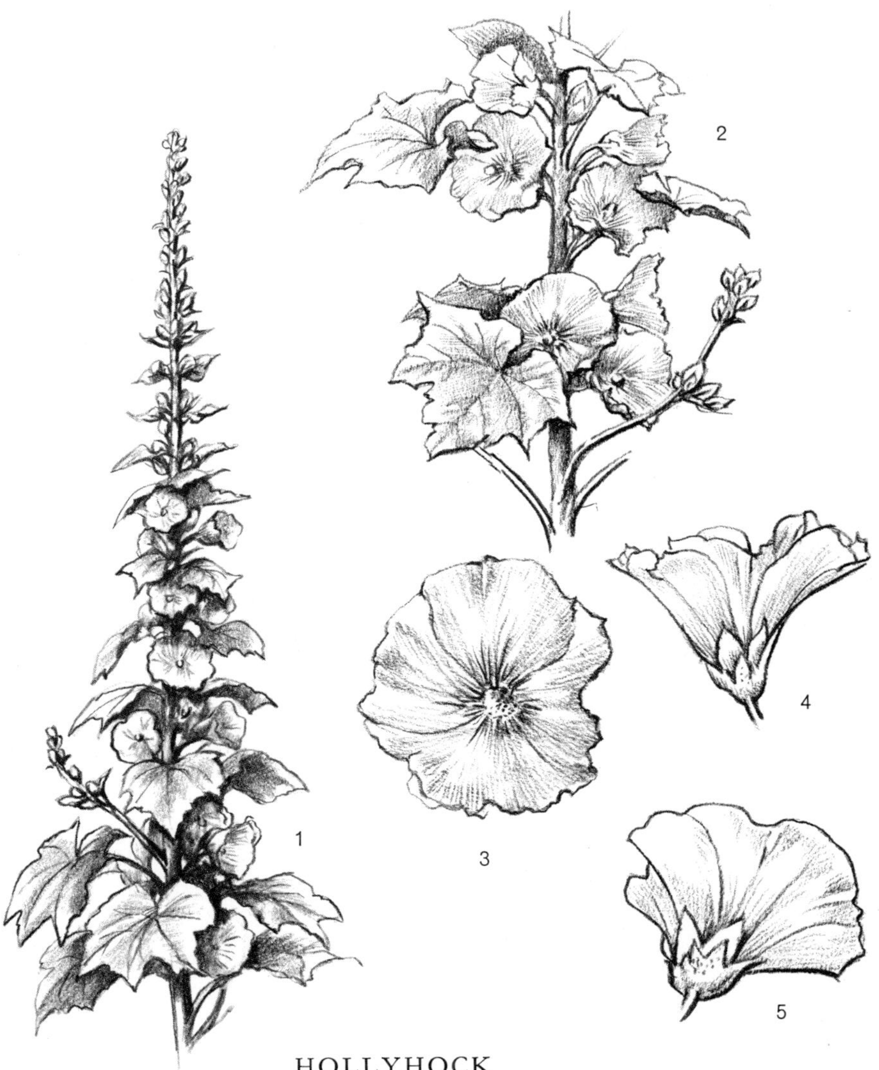

HOLLYHOCK

1 *Pyramid growth of the plant*
2 *Arrangement of leaves and flowers on stem*
3 *Single bloom, full face*
4 *Single bloom, side view*
5 *Single bloom, back view*

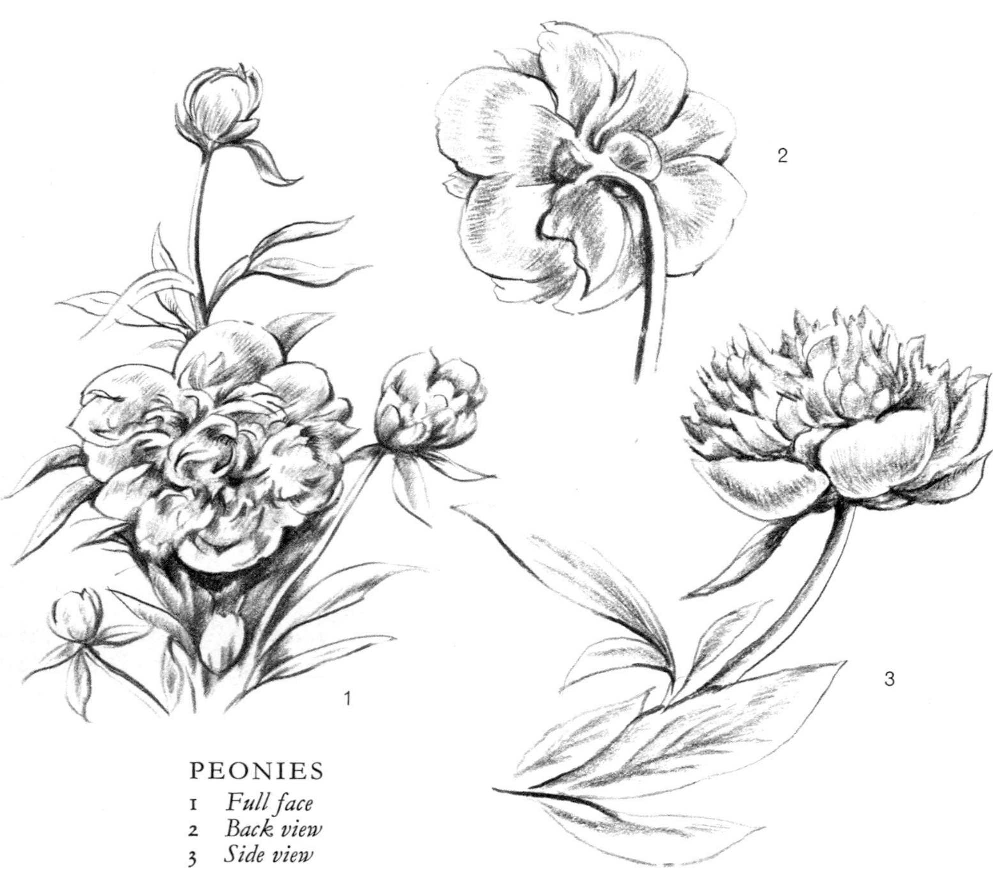

PEONIES
1 *Full face*
2 *Back view*
3 *Side view*

readers for whom this "*premier coup*" attack will make little or no appeal. It is, they may decide, too skilful, not to say, too much of a hit-or-miss technique, relying on its success by a dexterity of hand that may be thought beyond their attainment.

To those students I would suggest a watercolour *drawing*, where the colour is washed over a careful and complete drawing in a succession of transparent tints, which (as in this case speed is of little account) can be matched with loving regard for the original colour and shade of each particular flower.

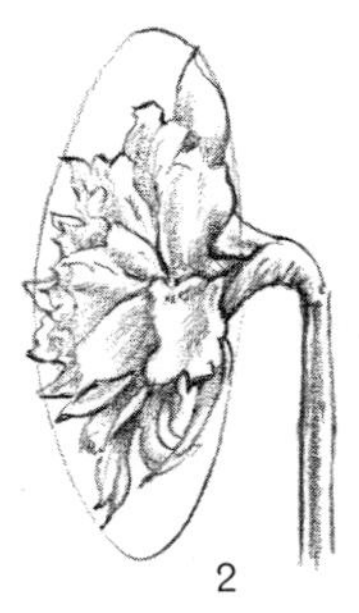

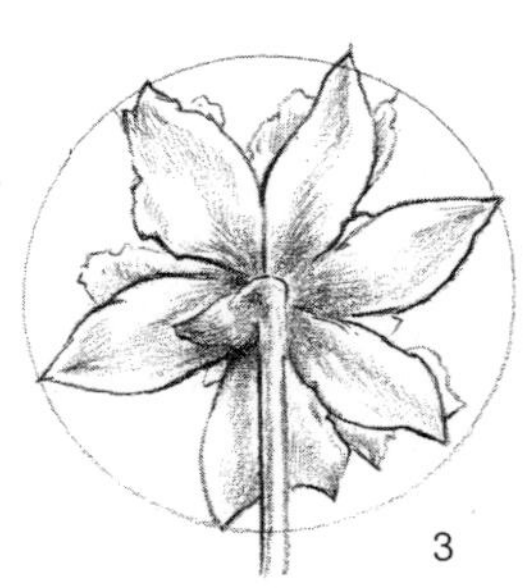

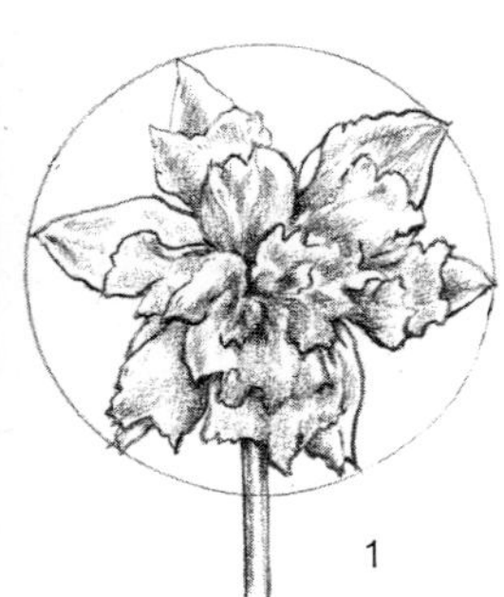

DAFFODILS

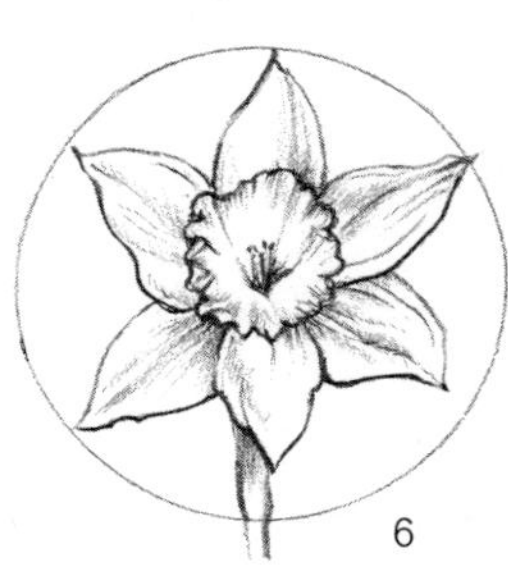

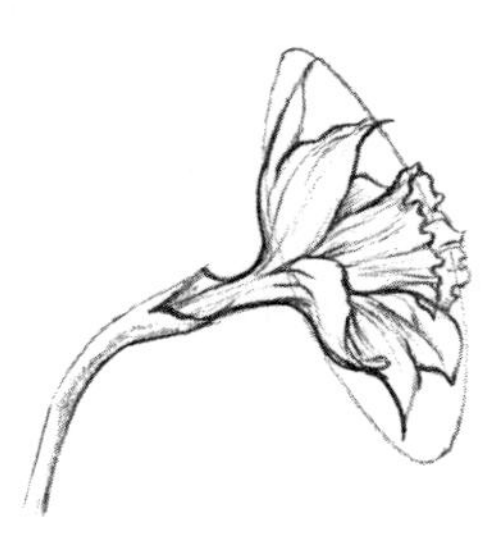

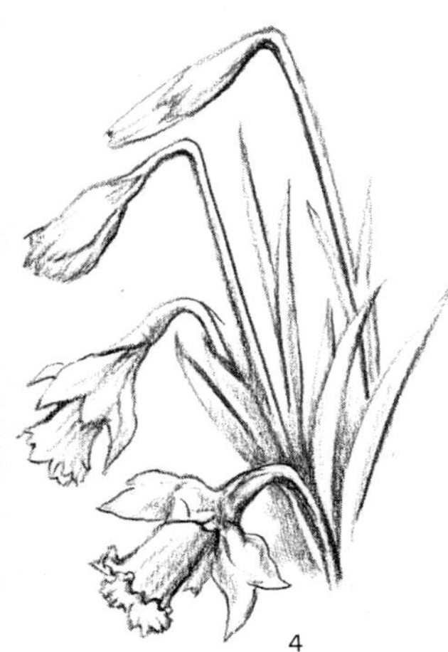

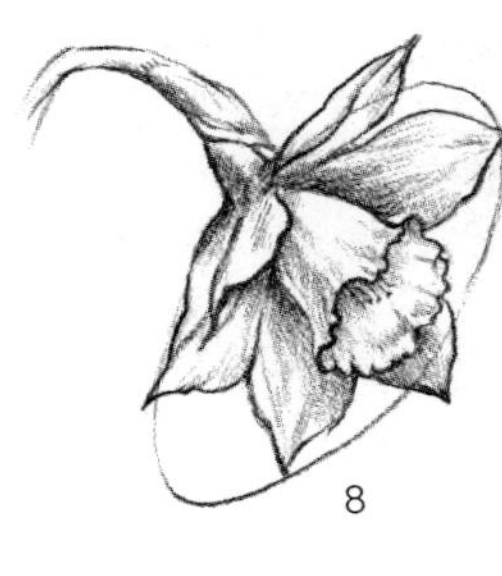

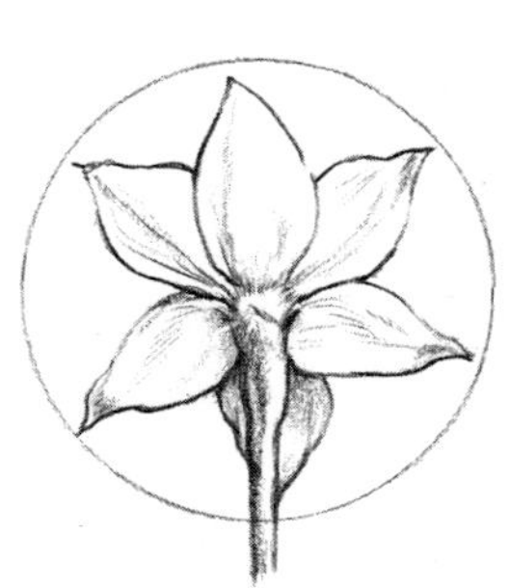

1 *Double Daffodil, full face*
2 *Side view*
3 *Back view*
4 *Four stages of growth*
5 *Single Daffodil, side view*
6 *Single Daffodil, full face*
7 *Single Daffodil, back view*
8 *Facing down*

Many beautiful flower paintings have been executed by such means. The precise delineation of each separate petal is preserved and the result makes a special appeal to discriminate and fastidious flower-lovers to whom technical verisimilitude is an essential quality for the lasting joy of contemplation.

I have myself devoted many happy hours of convalescence to this deliberate, leisurely and frankly loving approach to flower subjects! Some examples which I have chosen show the various styles I have adopted and the captions underneath, I hope, will supply sufficient information to enable the reader to follow, if desired, the same diligent pursuit of flower portrayal.

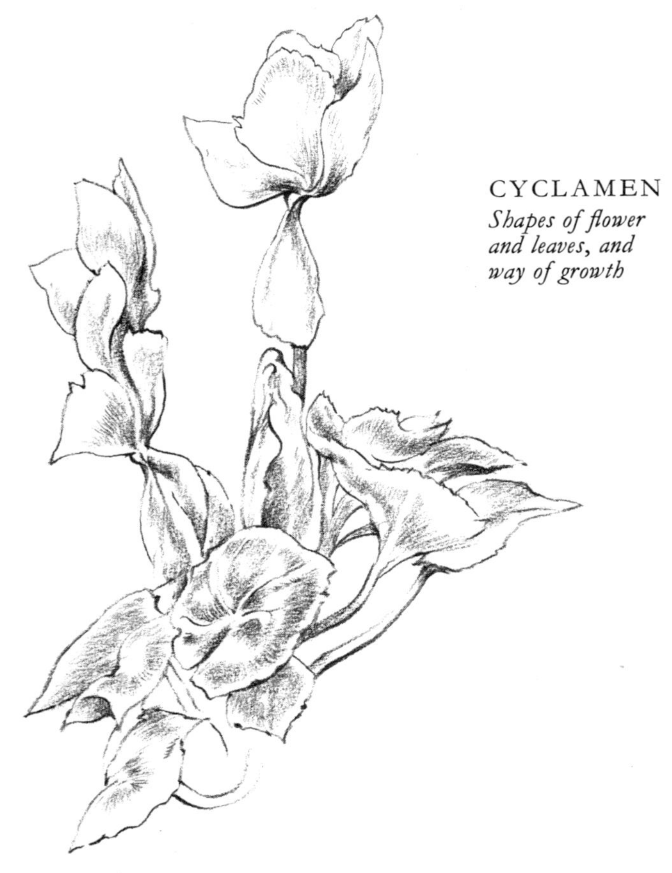

CYCLAMEN
Shapes of flower and leaves, and way of growth

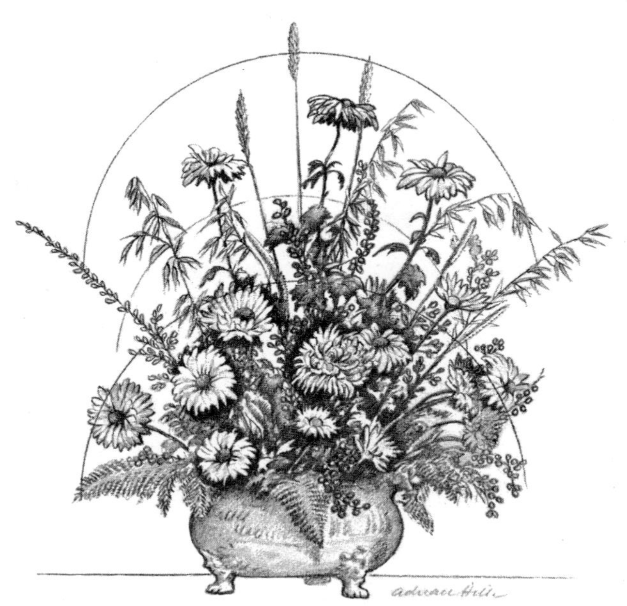

Note three directional lines for arrangement

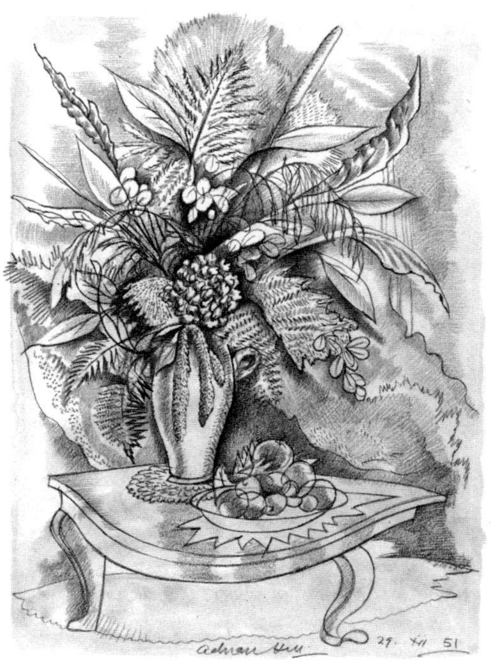

Personal technique

5: THE OIL MEDIUM

The plastic nature of oils lends itself admirably to many types of flower pictures in which textural quality as well as brilliance of colour, depth as well as design, completeness as well as effect are inherent in their technical attainment.

Certain flowers, moreover, especially those which in maturity achieve an obvious third dimension or "soft solidity", can only be properly depicted by a robust technique, which implies a generous use of the pigment. Fat (juicy is very descriptive) paint must in fact be used fearlessly if depth as well as wealth of colour is to be obtained. And as in most cases this desired effect can only be achieved by a succession of "sittings" it is in the oil medium, unlike that of watercolour, that successive stages—overpainting, repainting and glazing—can be indulged in without overtly impairing the textural quality nor in any degree lessen the spontaneity of the performance. Indeed, with a practised hand these deliberate processes can enhance the richness of the finished painting.

Canvas or board are equally responsive to this plastic treatment, especially when the palette knife is brought into play for purposes of heightening the impression of reality and giving emphasis in chiaroscuro or lighting.

And lighting, of course, should be one of our chief concerns, for by its use, we can pick out, subdue, reveal or discreetly subordinate those portions of our arrangement which can make or mar the desired effect.

Any attempt therefore at describing the successive stages of flower painting in oils must necessarily begin with this question of how to light our flower subject. (Hindsight is the privilege of all who can be said to have survived and benefited from the lessons of flower painting, and lighting is certainly one of them.)

Don't just paint any vase of flowers wherever it may happen to be seen. Try it out, here or there, in a corner, facing a window

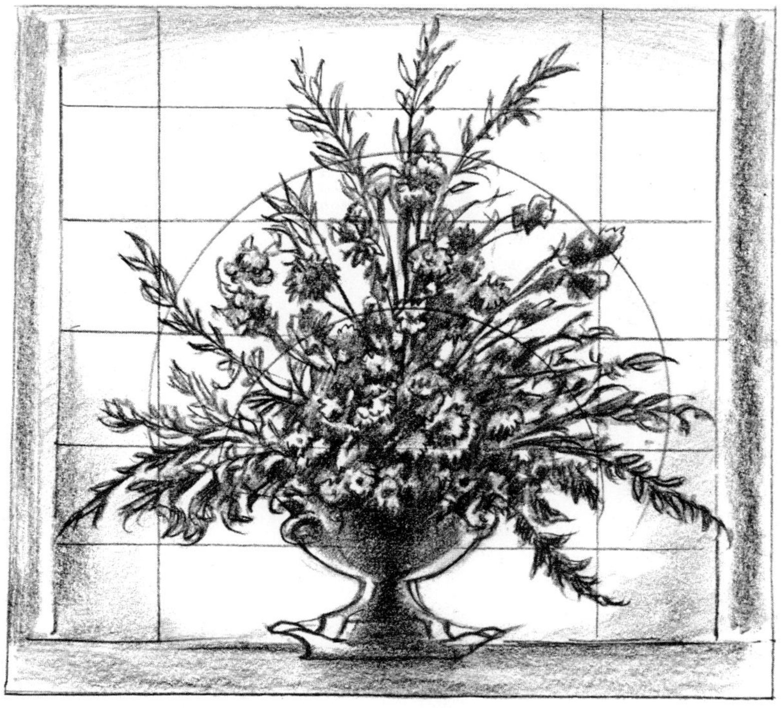

Against a window. (Suitable for oil technique.)

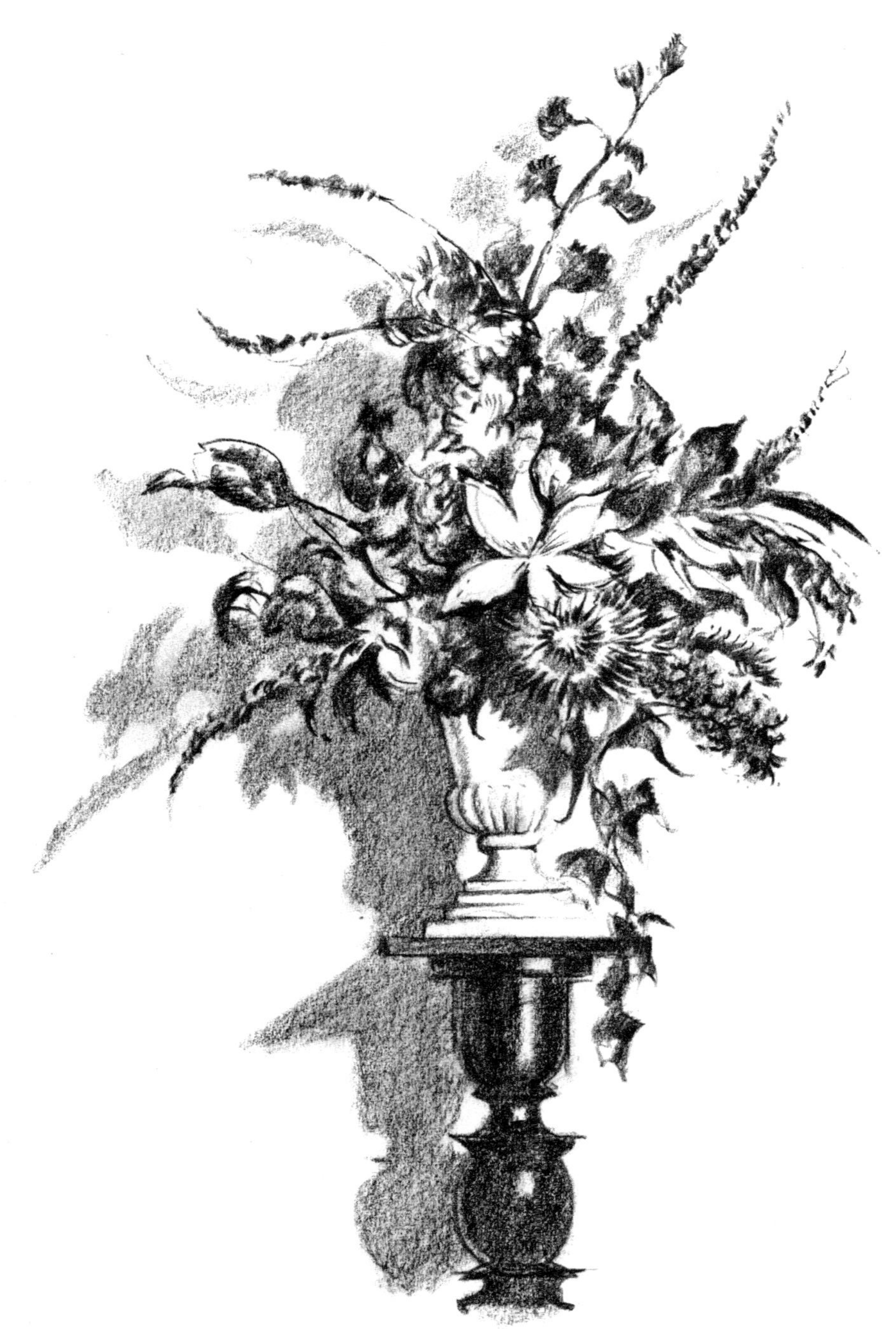

Shadows which help the composition

against a window or a curtain; because by moving it about and on different levels, you will discover how much difference lighting can make to your flower group.

I think the student will find that generally speaking flower pictures compose more satisfactorily as uprights than horizontal compositions, except when the arrangement is conceived in a shallow bowl or basket. These latter containers are particularly well suited for an arrangement of flowers painted in a modern idiom, as they offer plenty of scope for an imaginative display, which agrees well with modern techniques. For flower pictures, if truly contemporary in handling, should be typical of the prevailing fashion in floral designs—which, thank heavens, have progressed a great way from just "putting flowers in a vase"! (Due credit however must be given to Fantin-la-Tour for first employing the basket container for at least one of his Rose arrangements.)

In order sometimes to prevent a too obvious portrait of a vase of flowers, introduce some other article—a pair of scissors—a gardening glove, anything that looks natural and not affected (as the fallen flower beside the vase!).

Flower paintings, let us be frank, can be dreadfully conventional in composition, and it pays well to seek some fresh arrangement, which may be obtained as I have already suggested, by placing the flowers on a shelf—in an alcove—on a low stool—or even on the floor—anywhere in fact than always on the highly polished table top!

Having settled these points, and that of size and whether it is to be an upright or a horizontal shape (most important), you can start drawing in your design with a stick of charcoal—and a clear conscience! While it is not necessary to leave a margin *all round* the outside of your flower design, it is important to see that the composition does not appear cramped, as it assuredly will if all the outside flowers or leaves are painted right up to the top and sides of your picture. By all means let *some* of the foliage go out of the picture, especially at the top, but if you allow this to

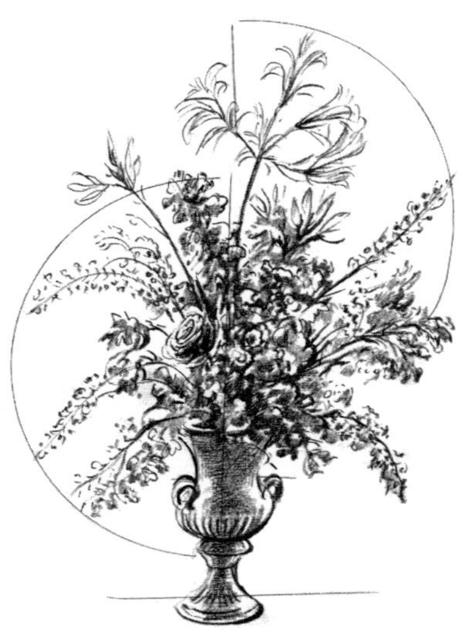

Traditional arrangement for urn container

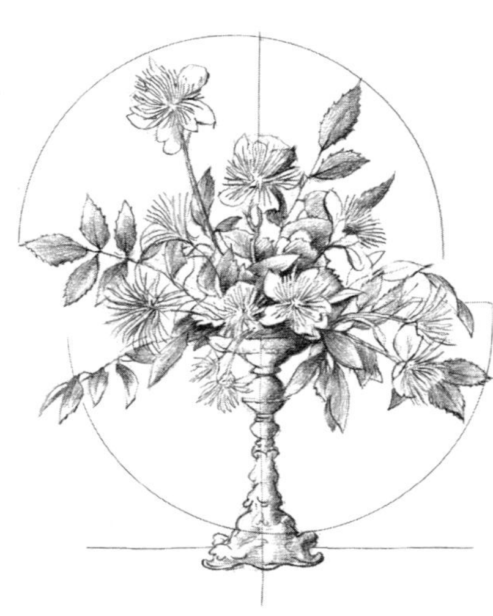

Novel arrangement appropriate for container

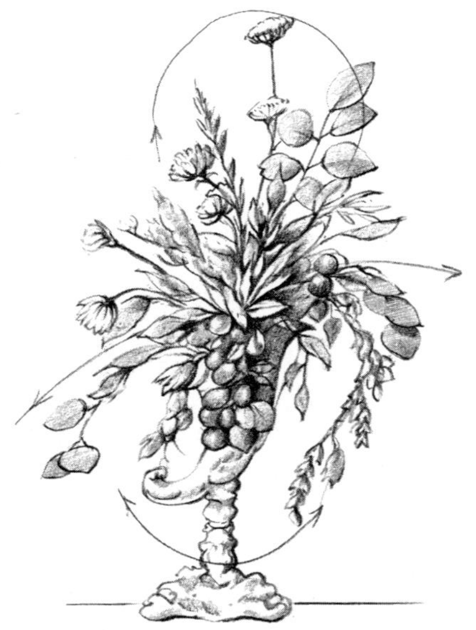

Contemporary design to harmonize with cornucopia shape of container

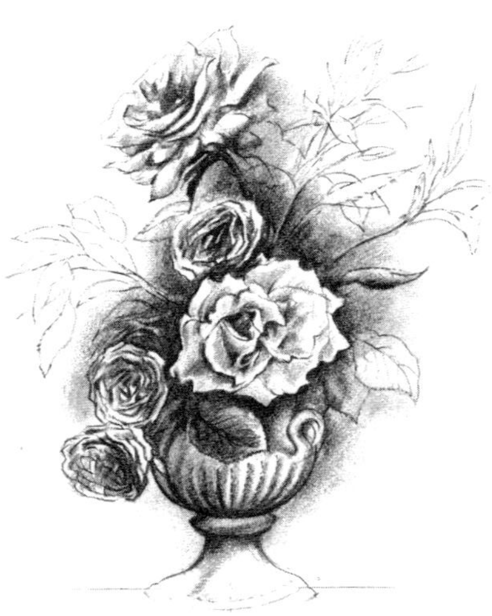

Suitable container for Rose design

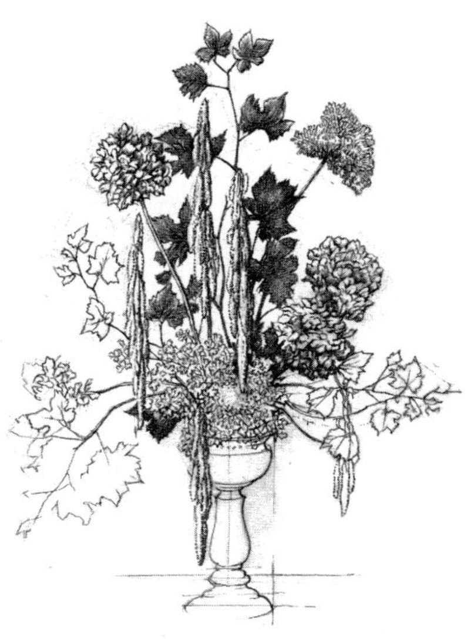

Austere and decorative

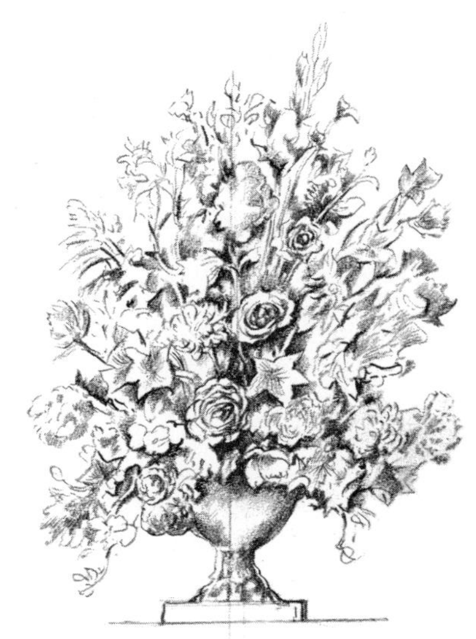

Grandiose effect

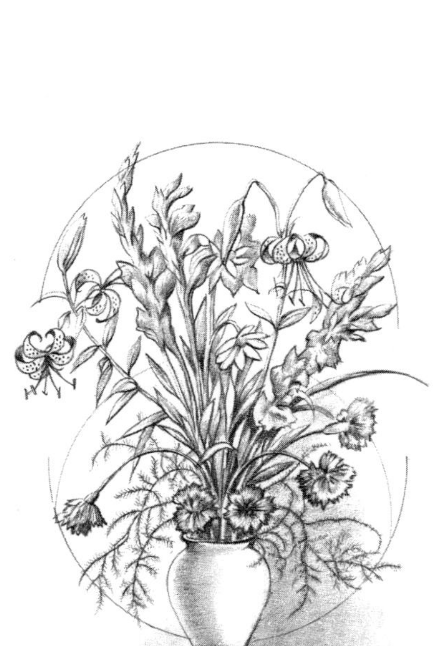

Formal arrangement

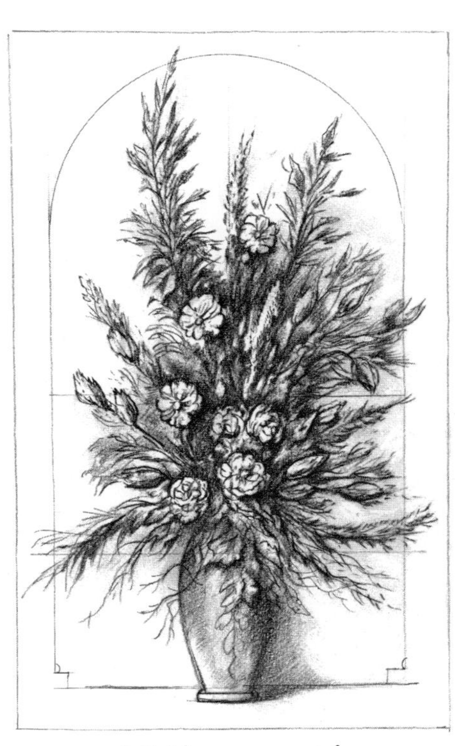

Suitable arrangement for an alcove

happen all round the sides of your canvas or board, your painting will most likely look like a detail of a larger picture. In upright subjects, where a tallish vase is used, see that the top of the container does not come more than half-way up your picture, and also that the background line which marks the boundary of the table top behind the vase does not come more than half-way up the side of the vase. And in horizontal subjects where *bowls* of flowers make the composition, the same warning is equally, if not more, important, for in horizontal flower pieces the flowers themselves must have as much room as possible to avoid a feeling of pictorial claustrophobia.

Your drawing should be firm and accurate and should include a broad indication of the light and shade, as this will indicate what your painting will add up to in terms of tone. Do not hurry this but clear up all doubts as to proportion and pattern, for in this stage you can alter easily by dusting off your charcoal and re-drawing where adjustment is required. This scaffolding can now be fixed (with fixative).

And now to the painting. From the colour range you intend to use, choose an earth colour, raw umber or sienna, and with plenty of turps, brush in the design so as to preserve the main construction and with sufficient pigment to cover the canvas or board. Use a large brush for this purpose. From now on you will be using less turps (linseed oil can be used with your turps) and more pigment, gradually building up your painting in degrees of depth, starting with the most important flowers or bunch and working outwards, upwards and downwards, until you reach your background and your flower container, vase or bowl, on its support. In this way you will see more clearly how much you may wish to direct attention to the setting, which, if not controlled, can so easily get out of hand and dominate the interest. Focal attention must always be directed towards the flowers, all else must be subordinated to *supporting interest*.

A word about colour combinations might not come amiss at this point. For example, white flowers with their attendant green

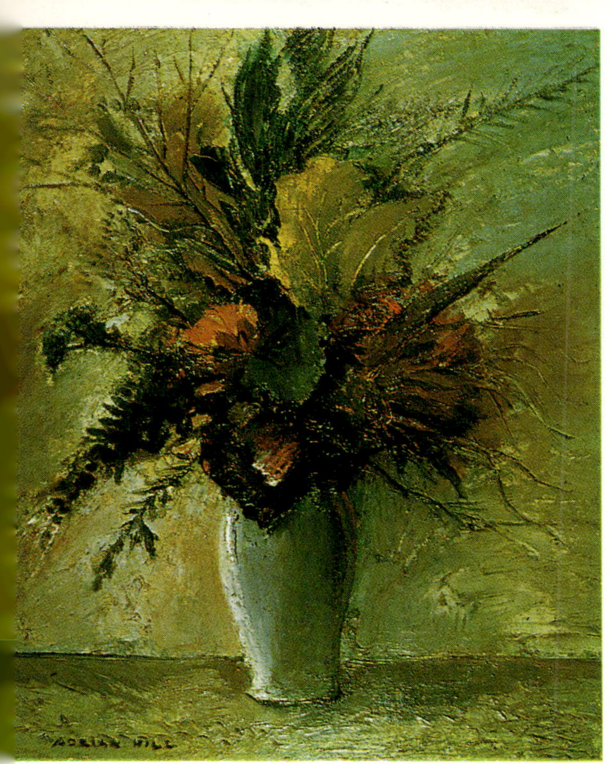

FLOWERPIECE
IN OILS
(In the collection of Andrew Faitlough, Esq.)

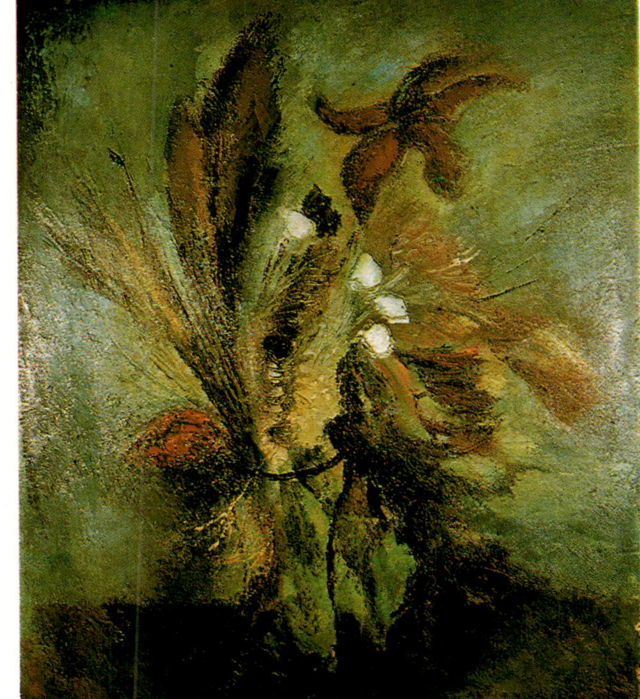

FLOWERPIECE
IN OILS
(Private collection)

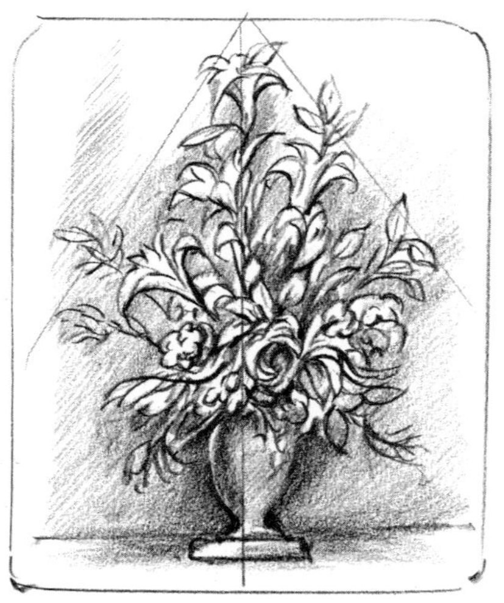

Facing the light—pyramid design

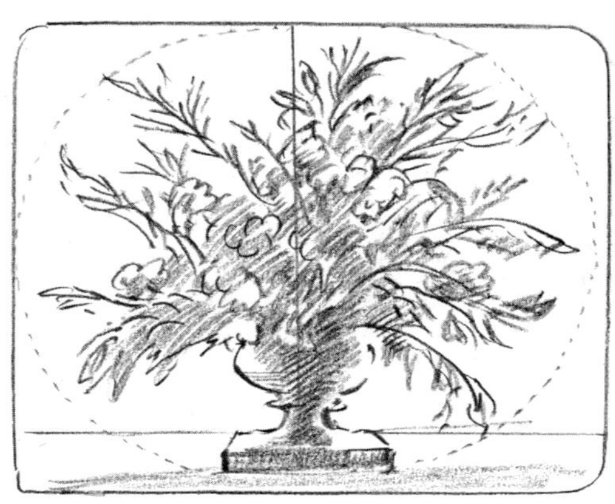

Light from behind—design within the ellipse

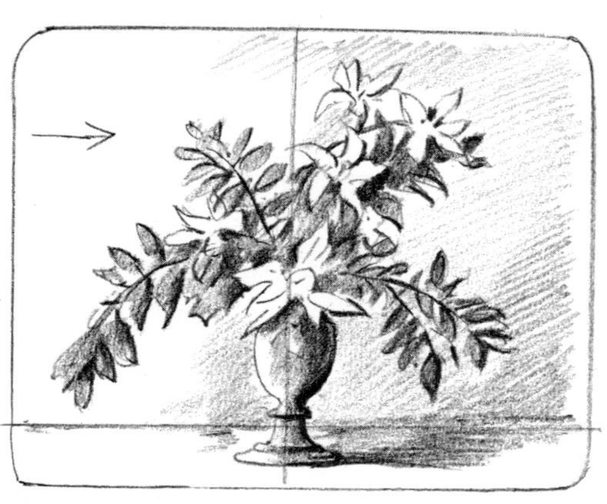

Strong light from the left

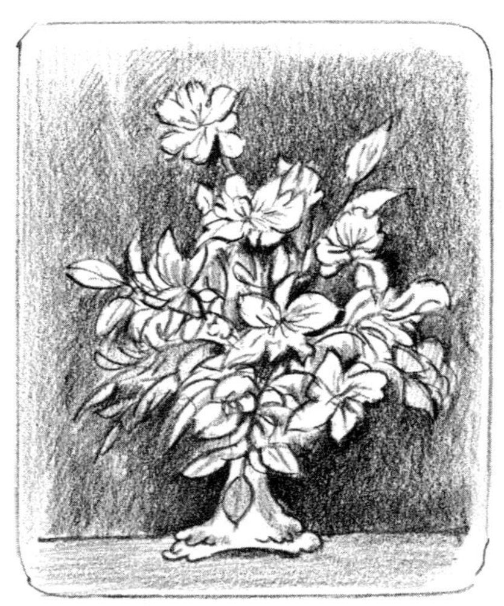

Silhouetted against a dark background

foliage can be ruined by a hot background and a coloured china vase. Red and yellow blooms mixed together unless the reds are muted and the yellows of a light tone, can be unhappy companions. Moreover, Daffodils, of the shade of a vivid cadmium if mixed with pink or purple Tulips in a copper container on a highly polished oak table against a royal blue curtain, can well be a positive affront to the sensitive eye! Before embarking, therefore, on any arrangement where there is a profusion of mixed flowers, all attempting to steal chief honours, it is advisable to choose, say a couple of Roses or Anemones in a simple jam-jar, so that your problems are limited to those of technique rather than the further complication of colour combinations and arrangement. Examples like these from the hands of such masters as Manet and Renoir will be of greater benefit than striving after the magnificent flower paintings of the early Dutch School. Simplicity can score over the grandiose, especially with flowers and certainly in the early stages of study.

Certain it is that once this medium has been mastered, the fugitive charm of flowers, the delicacy of their forms, clarity of colour, gossamer texture and subtlety of configuration as well as their third dimensional properties—all indeed that make flowers flower—these attributes can be reproduced closer to the original in oils perhaps than any other medium.

And it is comforting to reflect that unless absolute verisimilitude is required (and as it ever?) the painter is at liberty to lower, heighten or even change the basic colour, if pictorial harmony be retained. A dark background is often preferred to a light one, but see that this is not painted too thickly otherwise a sense of depth and atmosphere will be lost. Your heaviest impasto must be kept for those flowers which will make "the eye" of your composition. This is where glazing at a later stage can be so useful in giving a softening glow to a particular portion which may appear too light. The necessary tint is floated on like a watercolour wash with a soft *clean* brush. Do not, however, attempt to glaze until the surface you intend to soften is *quite* dry. And finally, do not be tempted to varnish your painting for at least a couple of months. Then use Mastic varnish and apply with a circular movement (either with a soft brush or a pad of cotton-waste) to the surface of the painting which should be laid in a horizontal position where it should remain until the varnish is dry.

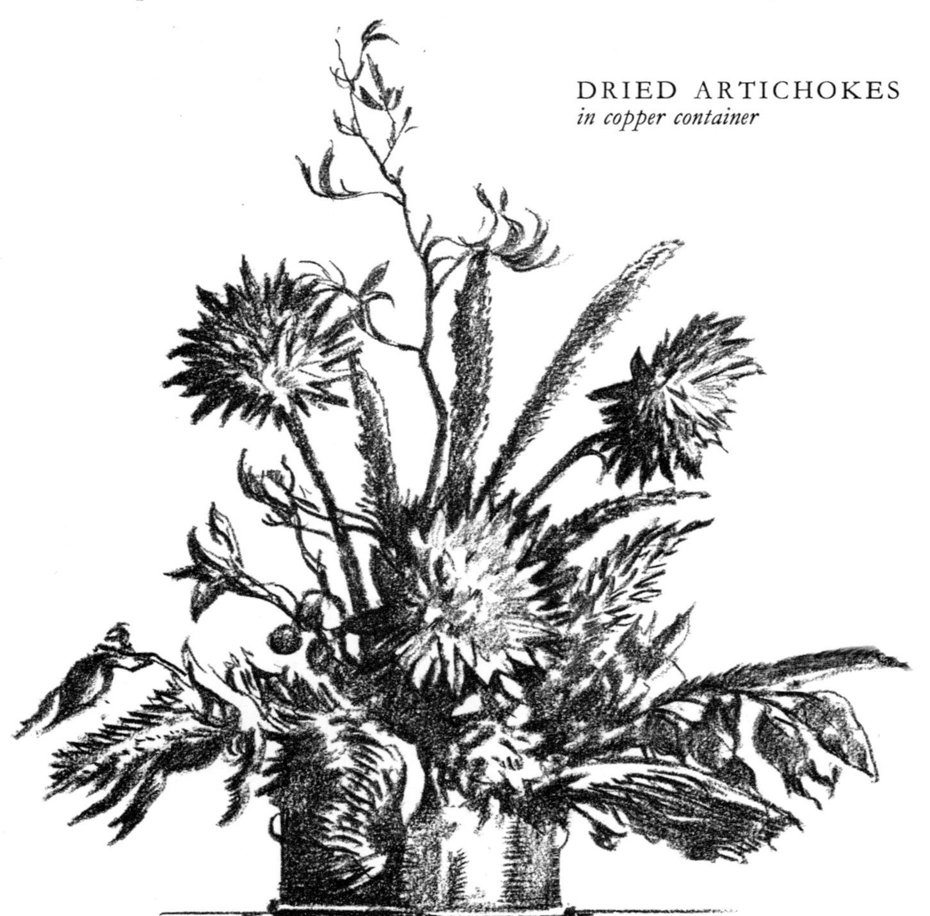

DRIED ARTICHOKES
in copper container

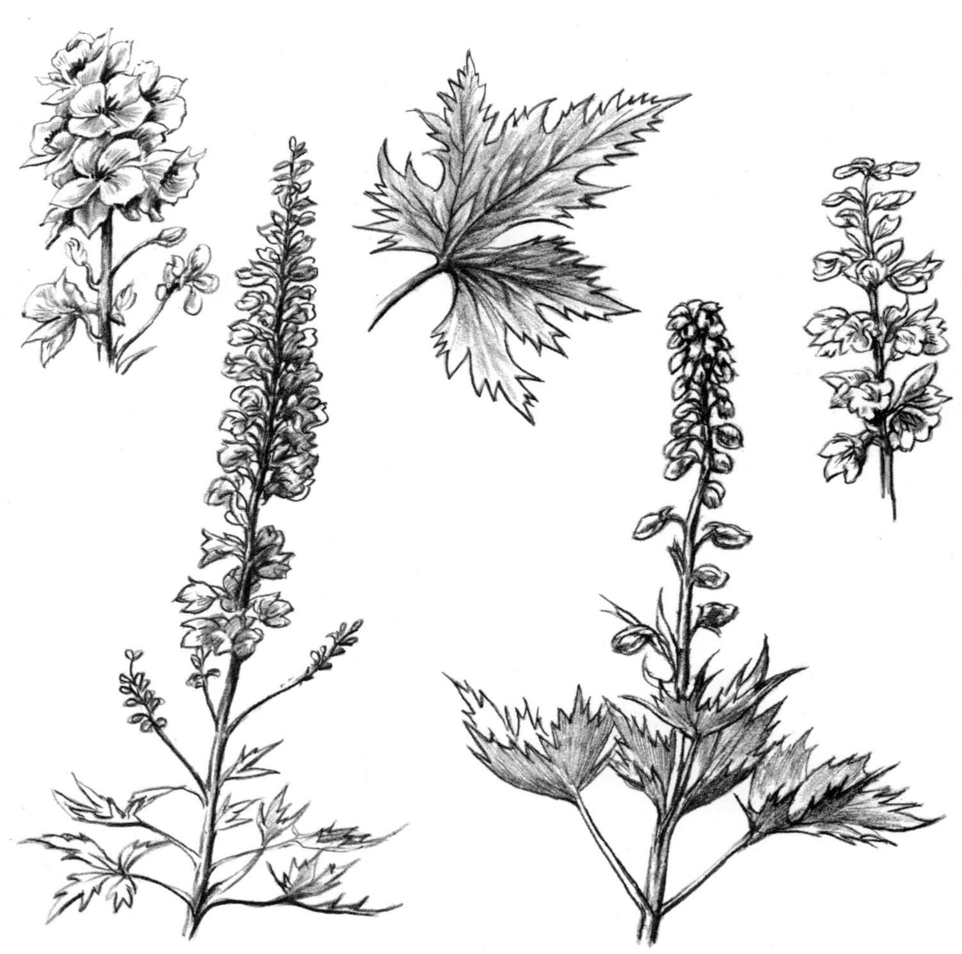

DELPHINIUMS *with details of flowers, leaves and early buds*

Here then we have two main approaches to flower painting: the transparent and the opaque, both of which the reader can take up with real enjoyment for, as I have tried to show, they range from the purely factual to the purely personal.

6: COLOUR PROBLEMS

It has been recognized and accepted that the unique coloration of certain flowers, in their sheer brilliance as well as in their translucent texture and hue, still appear to defy the skill of the manufacturer to match the colour with exactitude.

In my own experience there is a peculiar shade of heliotrope which has no equivalent in terms of pigment. Purples, violets and certain shades of scarlet are in this category where transparency is unavoidably lacking. But this handicap only makes the task more worthwhile and rewarding because as I have mentioned earlier, we have to compromise and get round our difficulty by adjusting adjacent colours which by modifying their brightness, will in juxtaposition, serve to heighten the brilliance of the colour desired. Having said that, out of the following list of special colours I hope the reader may find some distinctive tint which has proved elusive in matching the coloration of some special flower.

In watercolours, there are (in addition to Alizarin Crimson and Vermilion): Crimson Lake, Cadmium Red, Cobalt Violet, Violet Alizarin, Scarlet Alizarin, Rose Madder, Purple Lake, Rose Doré.

And in oils: Roman Ochre, Geranium Lake, Mars Violet, and Scarlet Lake.

Lampblack, Brown Madder, Emerald and Cobalt Green, and Monastral Blue can be obtained in both mediums.

It must be clearly understood that I am not advocating these colours for general use, but only for very special occasions, because if included in your ordinary range, these "synthetic" tints will cause havoc with the tonal quality of your painting, for the attainment of which the fewer colours you use the better.

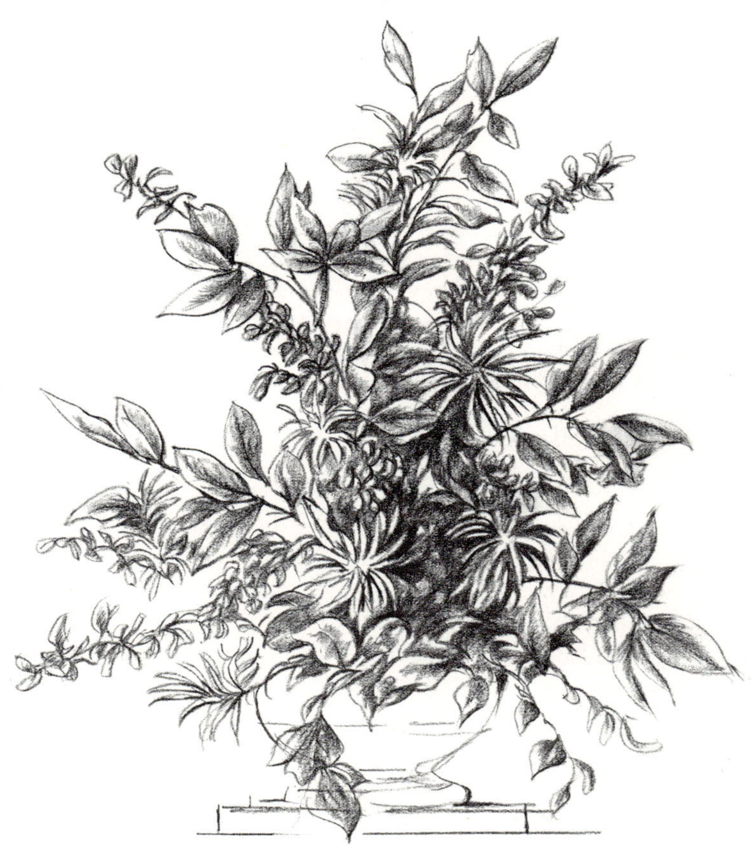

Tinted drawing

7: STOCK IN TRADE

If one possesses a garden, however small, the advantages of growing one's own particular flower models is self-evident, not the least advantage being that they can be cut as you want them and, being fresh, will last longer than those purchased in a shop.

In submitting the following list of flowers suitable for painting in either medium, my comments are those of the painter and not of the expert florist or plantsman!

Dahlias—Lend themselves well to decorative painting. Good models for slow workers, lasting a long time if the stems are dipped in boiling water.

Gladioli—Can be both large and opulent or delicate and dainty. Useful for a vertical composition.

Peonies—Long lasting, both single and double varieties. In maturity can resemble a full-blown rose.

Asters—Good range of colours.

Rhododendrons—The large-flowering evergreen foliage is in many shades and colours.

Magnolias and *Camellias*—Particularly attractive in single branch or flower form for specimen or decorative painting.

Irises—Available in other colours than blue.

Lilies—Arum, Madonna, Tiger and Auratum, all suitable for decorative flower pieces. Dark backgrounds are suggested.

Poinsettia—An exotic flower of distinctive shape and brilliant red colour.

Roses—Very paintable in both mediums from tight bud to full maturity.

Scabious—Distinctive flower in its shades of off-blue.

Sweet Peas—Lend themselves in bulk to an Impressionistic treatment.

Tulips—Very accommodating to modern approach and technique, especially in oils.

Zinnias—Like the Dahlias. Large range of strong colours.

Chrysanthemum—Lends itself better to an Impressionistic treatment than one that aims at detailed accuracy.

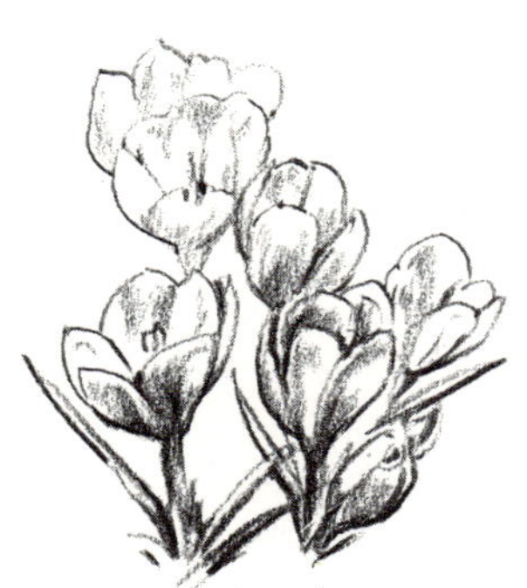

CROCUS

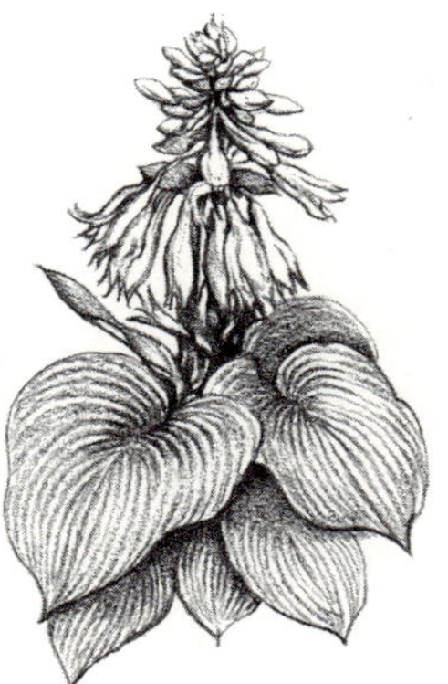

HOSTA

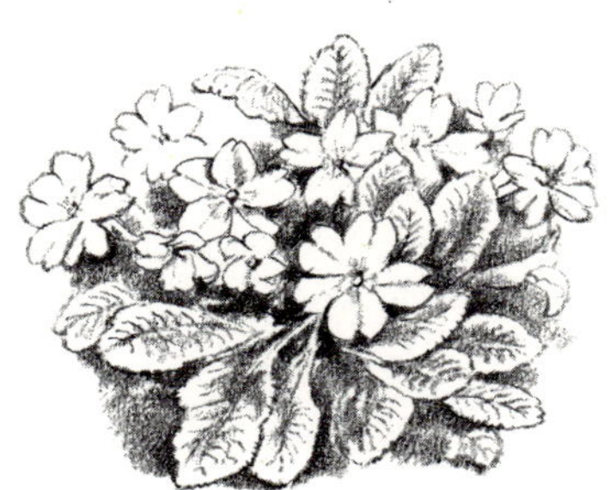

PRIMROSE

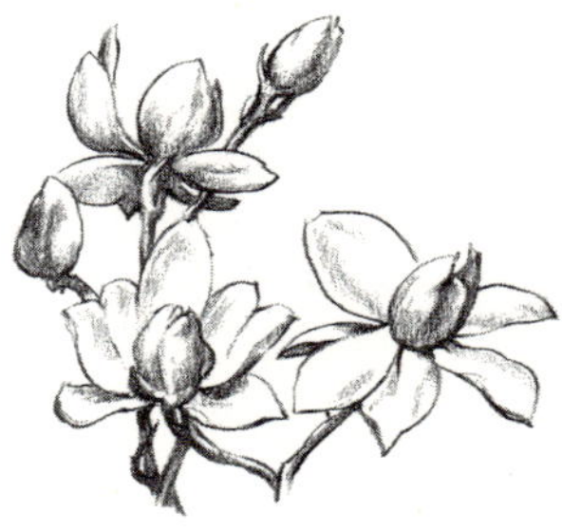

MAGNOLIA

Forsythia—Suitable for a decorative motif as flowers appear before the leaves.

Salvias—Good shapes and wide range of colours.

Carnations—Useful when used with other flowers as supporting colour interest.

Violets, *Lilies of the Valley*, *Primroses*, *Pansies*—Of compact growth and profusion of blooms. More suitable for miniature painting.

Cineraria, *Cyclamen*, *Begonia*, *Hyacinth*—Pot plants suitable for a botanical technique.

Daffodils, *Narcissi*—Because of their colour are more suitable for the watercolour medium.

Wallflowers, *Larkspurs*, *Stocks*—Useful shapes for supporting interest.

Nasturtiums—Their trailing quality is of pictorial value.

Fuchsias—Many varieties. A light and dainty type of flower. Specially good for tinted drawings.

Orchids, *Camellias*, *Gardenias*—Excellent for flower portraiture as tinted drawings.

Hydrangeas—In late autumn the flower clusters turn magnificent colours and when picked retain their various shades throughout the winter.

Delphiniums, *Lupins*—Now available in other colours than the "pretty" blue! Suitable for vertical compositions.

Anemones—Very paintable, with wide range of definite colours.

Honeysuckle—Offers many stylized and decorative motifs.

Poppy—A striking feature in a mixed group of flowers. Resembles a peony in its double form, when it can be used on its own.

Hosta—Perpendicular stem, bell shape flowers, in pastel colours with particularly paintable foliage.

Spring flowers, I should say, and those of tender shape and delicate colouring lend themselves more readily to the transparent medium of watercolour. Yellow, especially in this medium and in certain shades of blue in oils, should be used with discrimination if "prettiness" (see Delphinium "blue") is to be avoided! Finally

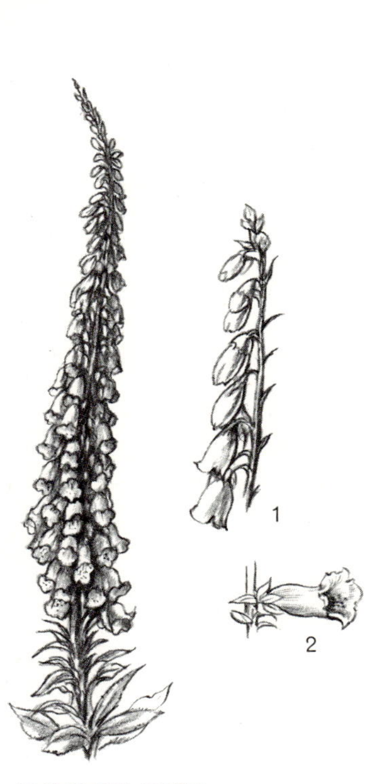

FOXGLOVE

1 *Buds*
2 *Details of flower*

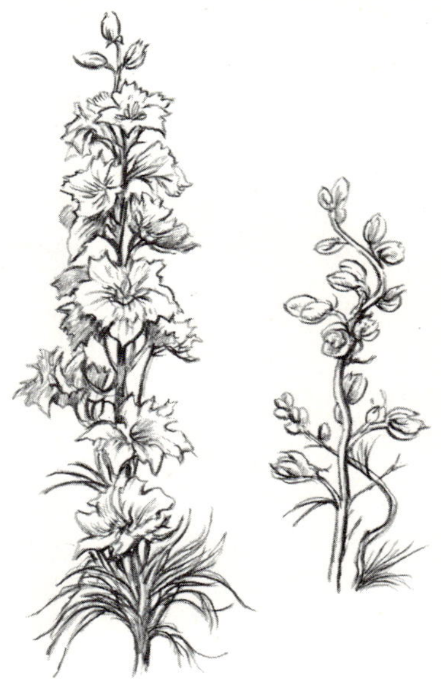

LARKSPUR

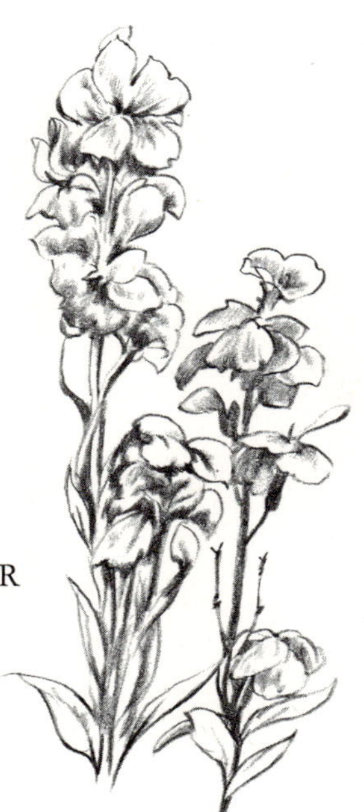

WALLFLOWER

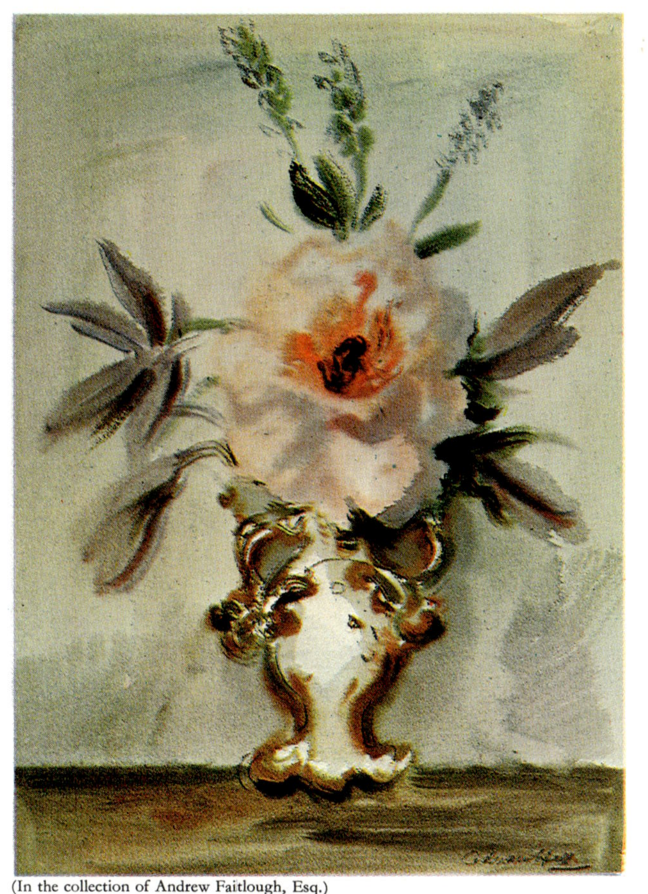

(In the collection of Andrew Faitlough, Esq.)

PORTRAIT OF A FULL BLOWN ROSE

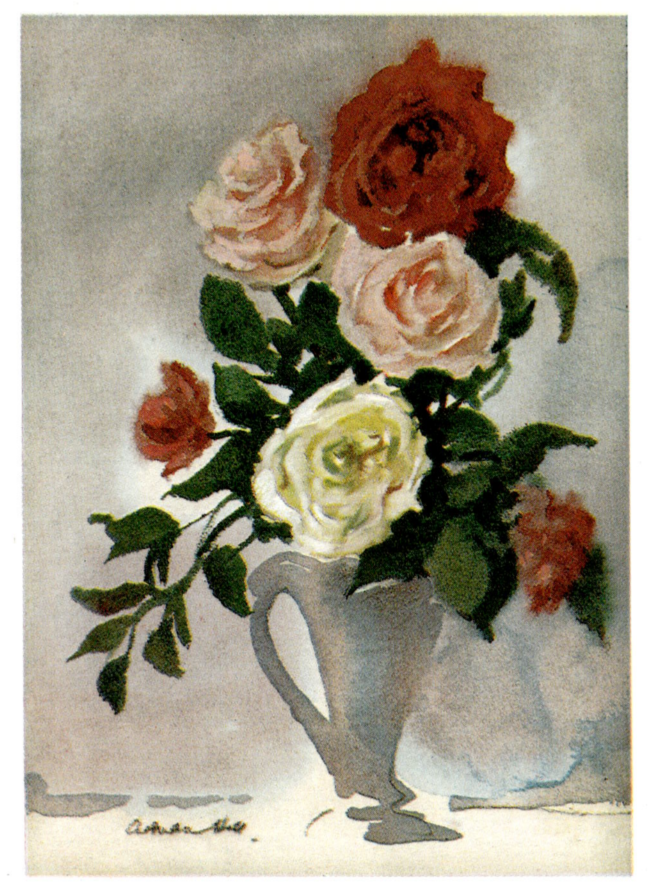

ROSES IN A VASE *Watercolour study*

boldness and direct handling in both mediums should be encouraged otherwise laboured "photographic" finish may defeat the aim of artistic integrity.

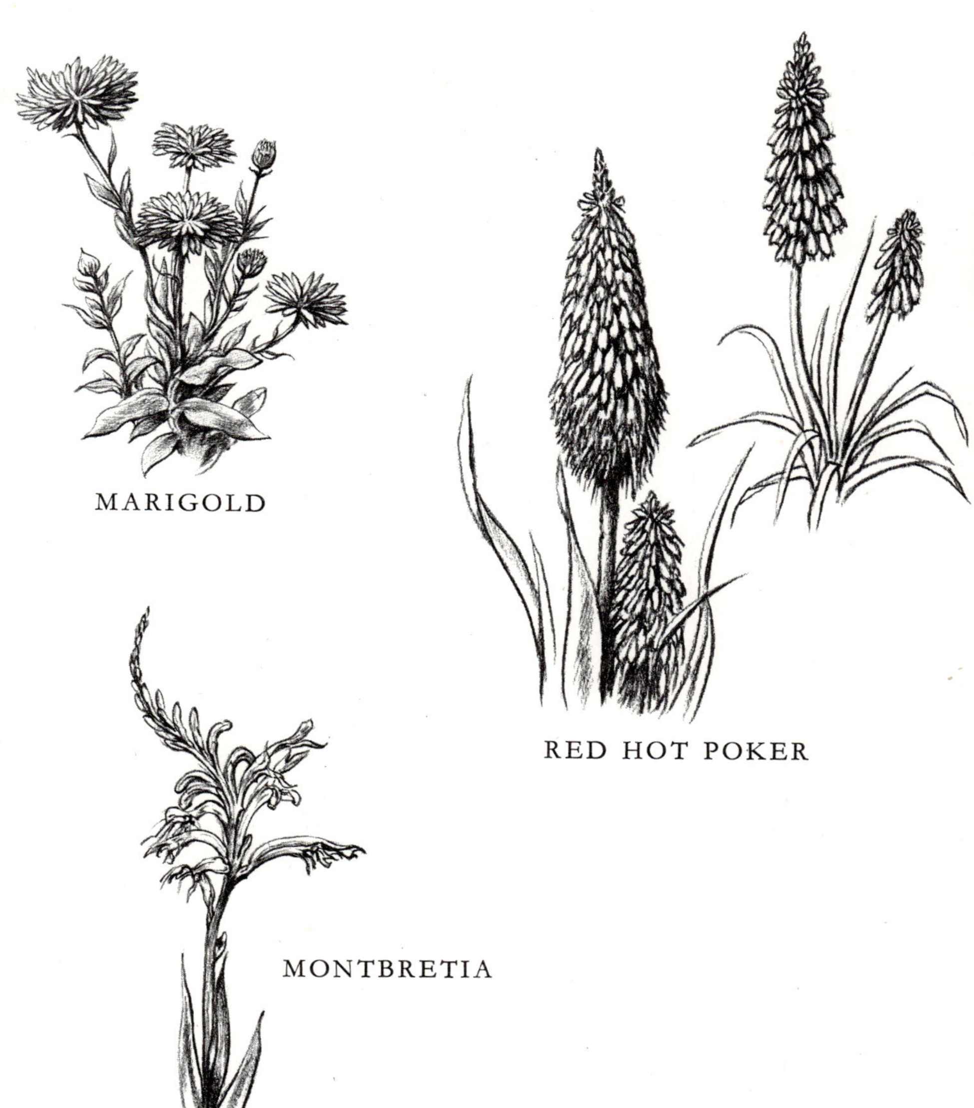

MARIGOLD

RED HOT POKER

MONTBRETIA

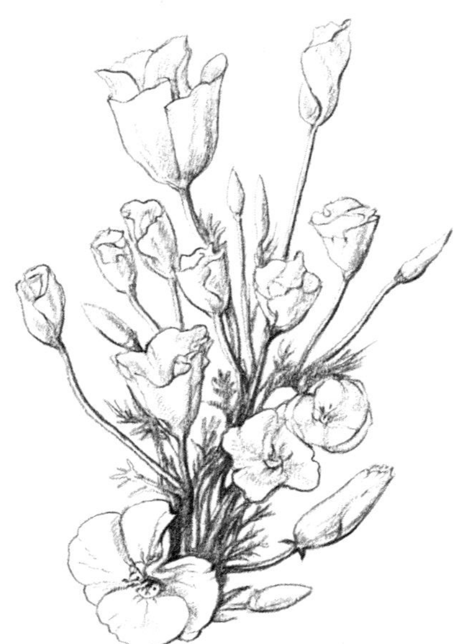
ESCHSCHOLTZIA

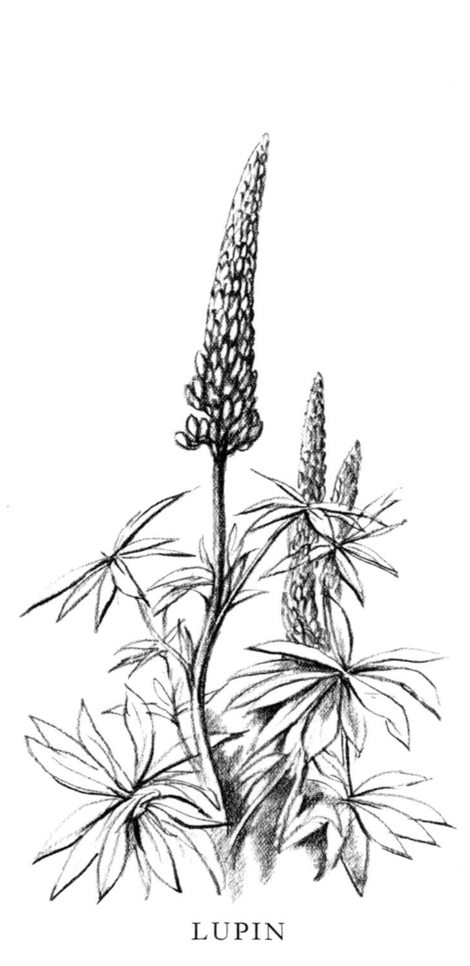
LUPIN

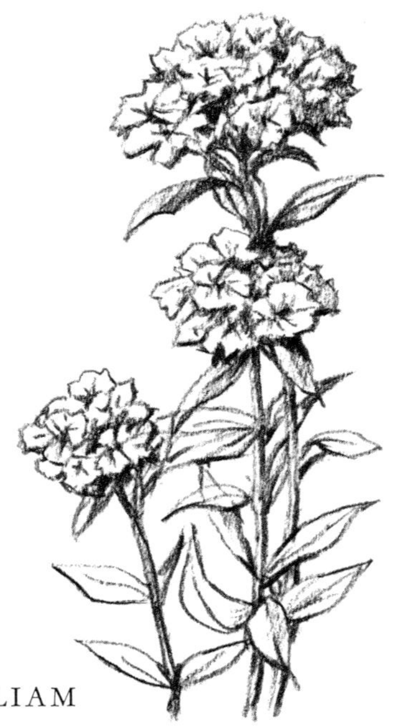
SWEET WILLIAM

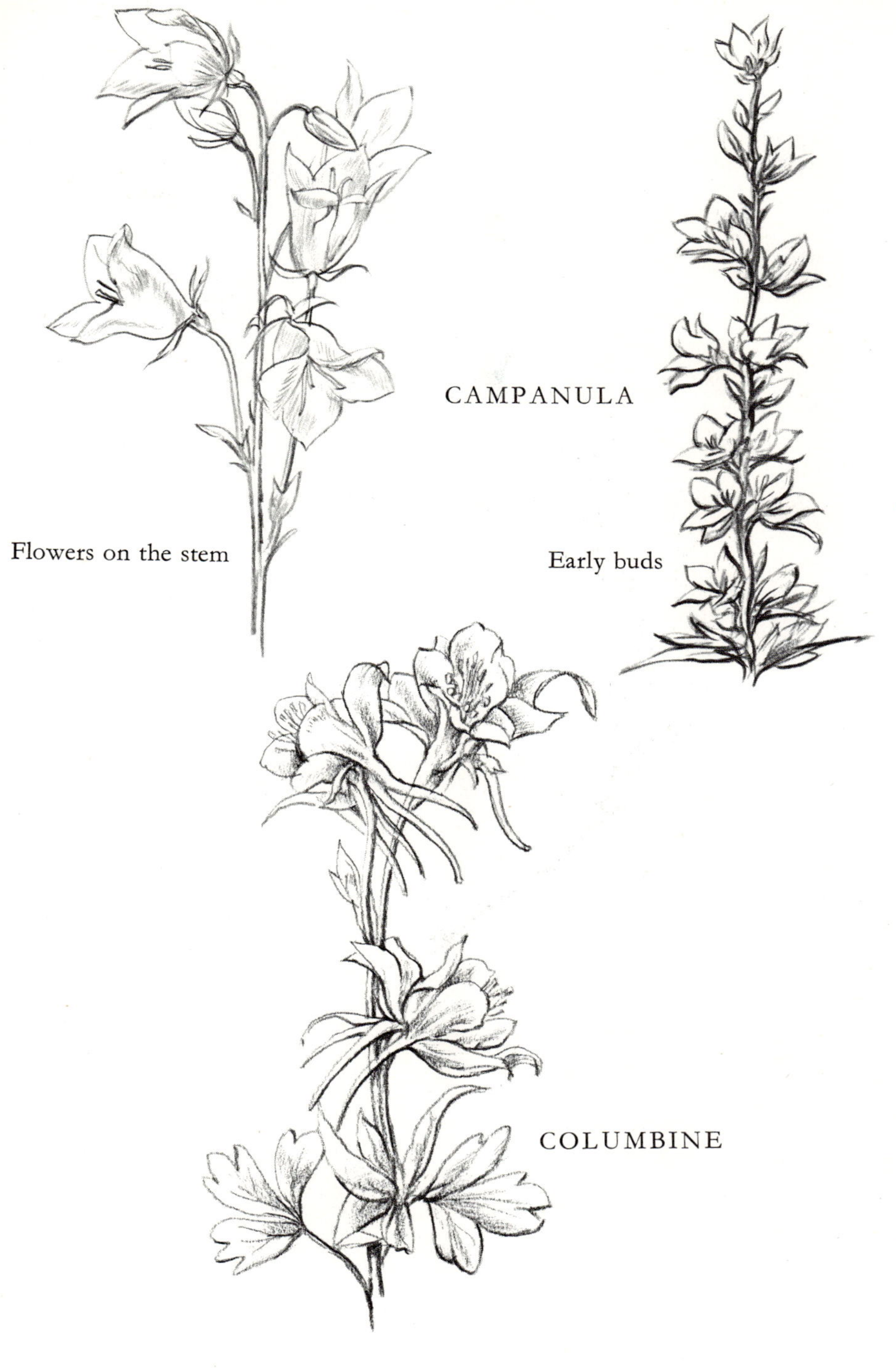
CAMPANULA
Flowers on the stem
Early buds
COLUMBINE

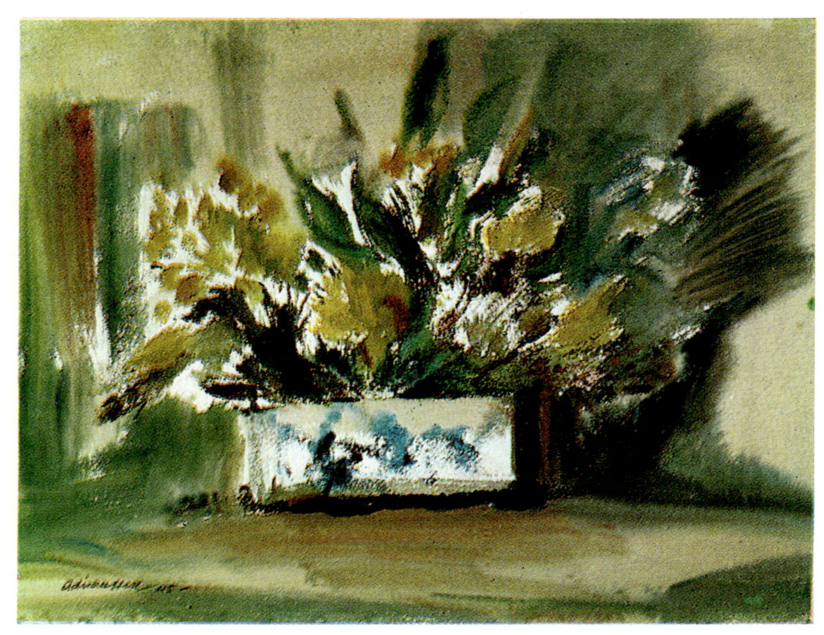

SPRING FLOWERS

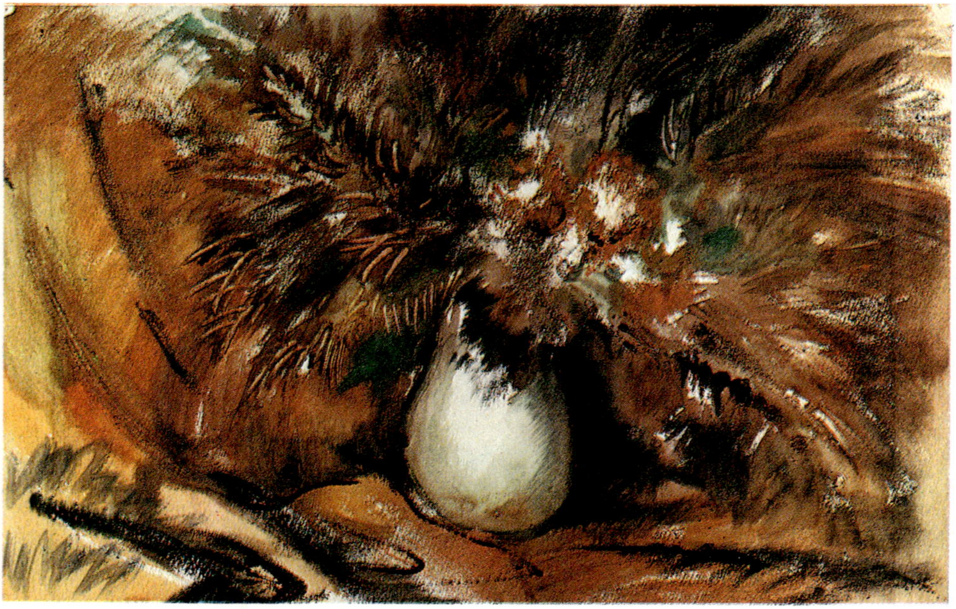

AUTUMN COLOURING

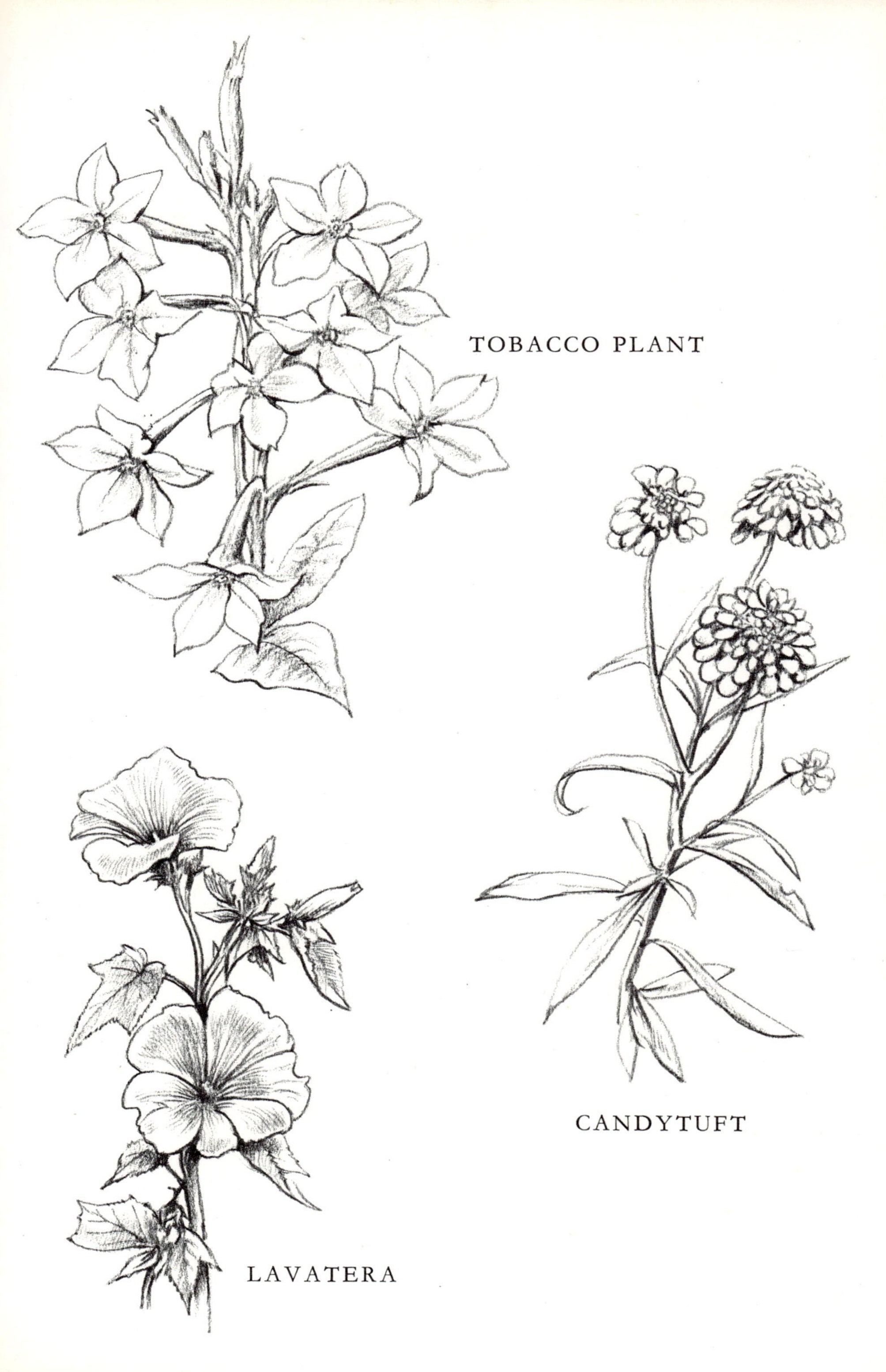
TOBACCO PLANT
CANDYTUFT
LAVATERA

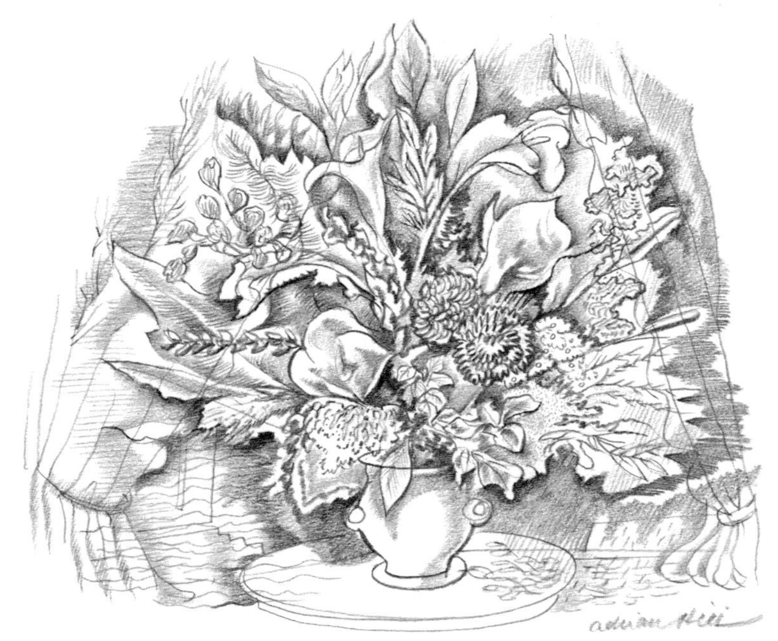

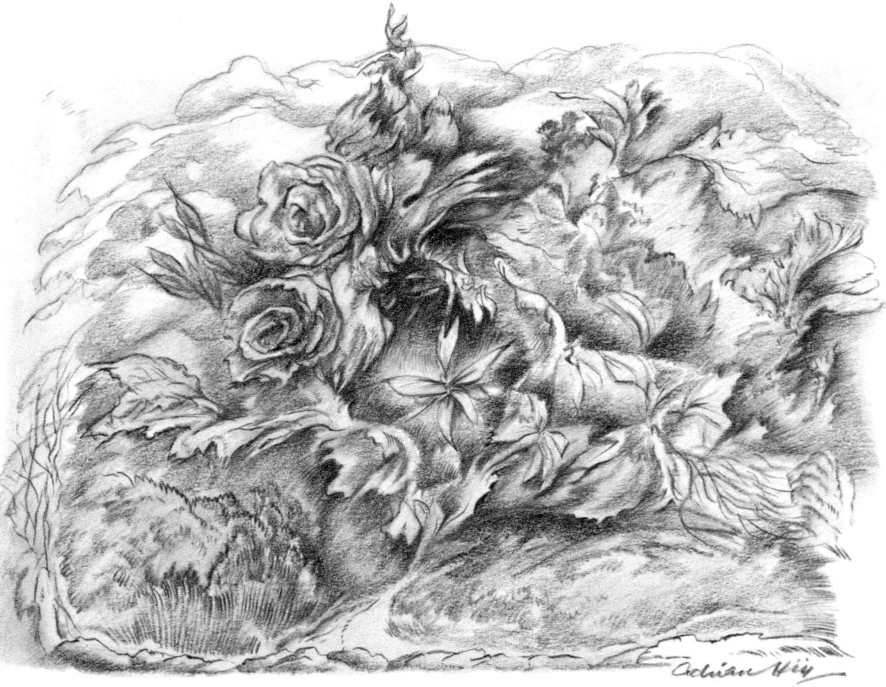

Flower theme

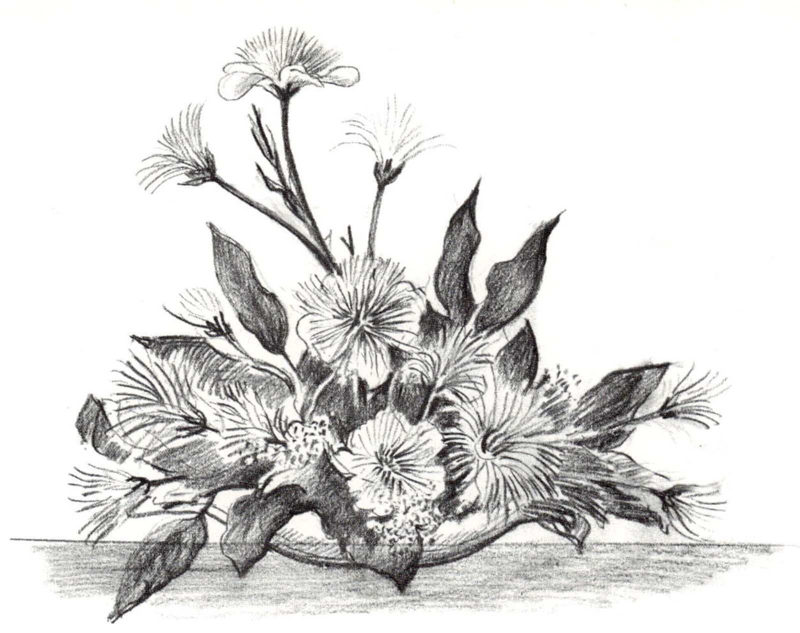

By the use of a shallow bowl, a lunette shape is achieved

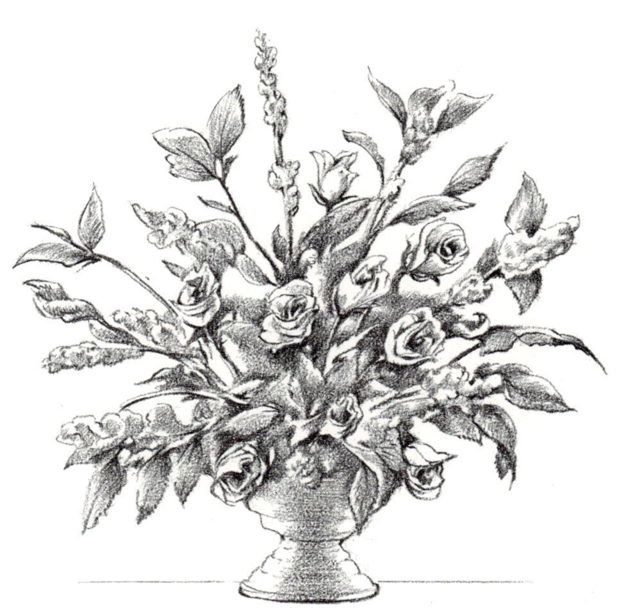

Note height and width of container with the height and width of flower arrangement

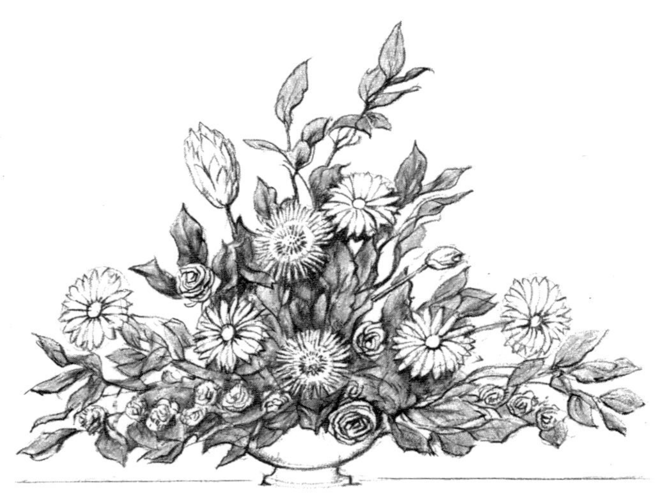

Strict decorative dried flower arrangement in a 'soup tureen' container

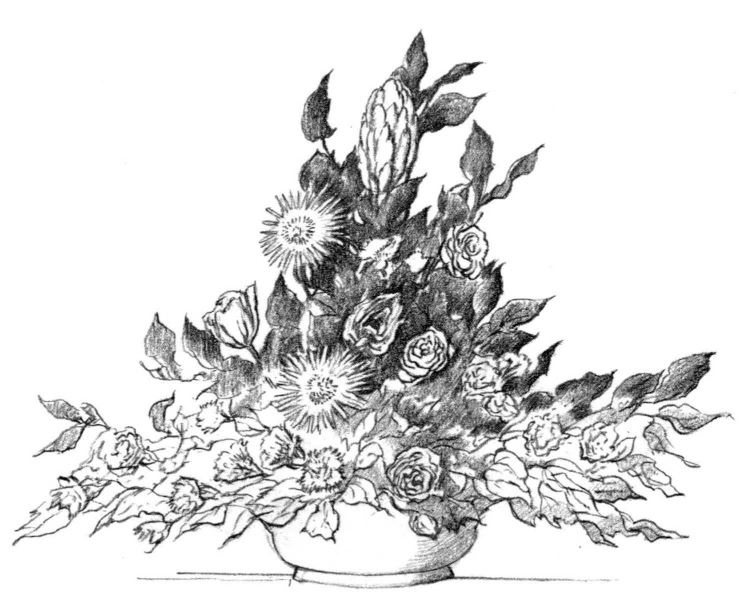

Note the serrated outline of the flower design with the curved shape of the bowl

8: CONCLUSION

How far is it possible or justifiable to translate and synthesize flower subjects into self-expressive paintings where the flowers themselves are made obedient to the artistic whims of transmutation? This is a question which at one time or another the painter himself must decide.

I would venture that once (like all other forms in Nature) the characteristics of coloration of flowers and their way of growth, have been properly understood and mastered, the painter is free to indulge in whatever form of transfiguration (barring complete metamorphosis) he considers expedient to express better the abstract or lyrical possibilities which the flower world is capable of offering. Indeed, I would go as far as to say that as long as the result is pictorially acceptable—that which would exclude all flippancy or resort to shock tactics—there are no artistic boundaries beyond which the bold experimenter cannot go, for herein lies the right of the creative artist to explore and exploit his own individuality. Many of the accompanying illustrations will, I hope, show what I have attempted in extending my own range and portrayal of subjects in which flowers are the motif. It will be seen that such artistic licence is as much in evidence in the technical handling employed as in both the setting and in the actual flower formation. By such means the artist is exonerated from artistic smugness and from the danger of succumbing to the "fatal" charm which flowers can so easily exercise over the unwary. Oh, that deadly repetition of a well trained technical formula when the hand that wields the brush is restricted and performs almost mechanically and the inquisitive eye is bemused by regarding the present problem through the rosy glasses of past successes. Then it is that stern measures have sometimes to be taken to free the very flowers themselves from the cloying bondage of a "commercial" calendar prettiness. The reader, I'm sure, knows what I have in mind!

Indeed it is only with vigilance and in such a spirit of adventure that flower paintings can retain their pictorial significance and take their rightful place in this fast-changing world of contemporary art.

One final caution from Hugh Garden Porteus: "Yet an artist should be an explorer like Bach or Leonardo, alternately discovering, improving, and inventing, rather than a salesman, peddling a single line of goods." In this case "the line of goods" might well apply to flowers! We have been warned!

To sum up then: to paint flowers so that the beholder can identify the particular species may be thought a necessary obligation, but in fact it is not indispensable to the artistic merit of the painting. For in the last analysis it all depends *how* flowers appeal and what *you* want to say about them!

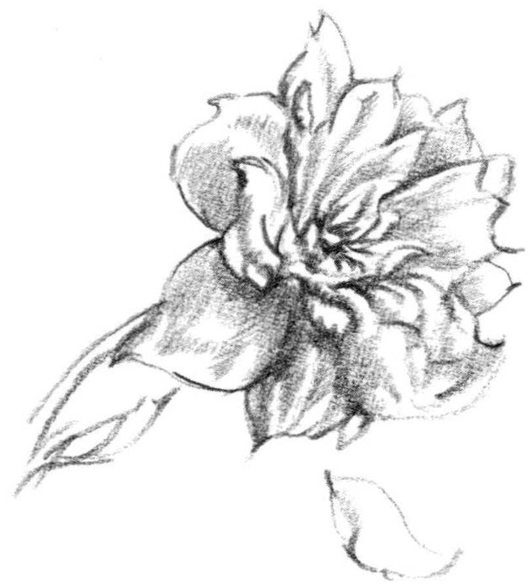